COME SHINING

COME SHINING

More Poems and Stories from Fifty Years of Copper Canyon Press

EDITED BY MICHAEL WIEGERS

AND KACI X. TAVARES

Copper Canyon Press

Port Townsend, Washington

Cover art: Erika Blumenfeld. *Encyclopedia of Trajectories: Untitled Meteors,* 2017, 10.25 × 14.25 inches, single-stroke drawings with finely ground 23.75 karat gold suspended in gum Arabic on 140-pound Arches Aquarelle hot-pressed watercolor paper. www.erikablumenfeld.com

Copper Canyon Press is in residence at Fort Worden State Park in Port Townsend, Washington, under the auspices of Centrum. Centrum is a gathering place for artists and creative thinkers from around the world, students of all ages and backgrounds, and audiences seeking extraordinary cultural enrichment.

The Library of Congress has catalogued this record under LCCN 2023021428.

ISBN 9781556596971 (paperback)
ISBN 9781619322875 (epub)

9 8 7 6 5 4 3 2 FIRST PRINTING

COPPER CANYON PRESS
Post Office Box 271
Port Townsend, Washington 98368
www.coppercanyonpress.org

Acknowledgments

Our original hope was that during our fiftieth anniversary we would be able to tell the history of the Press, and as always, poetry would be front and center in that history. But the response from our community was too meaningful to ignore, and in editing this supplementary companion volume, our hope is that we can not only acknowledge but also highlight the many brilliant minds flashing within our books. Throughout both *A House Called Tomorrow* and *Come Shining,* you will find the names of many of those who suggested poems and offered intimate, personal stories. We hope you will be as deeply grateful for their personal commitment and engagement as we have been.

The editors would like to express our deepest gratitude to Jay Aja, Jay Baker, Elizabeth Brueggemann, Asela Lee Kemper, Ivy Marie, and Azura Tyabji, whose invaluable contributions and persistence enabled the gathering and representation of the many stories, poems, and passions of the Copper Canyon Press community.

We would also like to thank our ever-patient and creative colleagues at Copper Canyon Press. Thank you to Joseph Bednarik and John Pierce, who contributed to the original envisioning of this book, and to Janeen Armstrong, Claretta Holsey, Marisa Vito, and Ryo Yamaguchi, without whom we could not have created *Come Shining* and its accompanying digital presence on our website. Our heartfelt thanks also extends to the rest of the Copper Canyon staff and to Valerie Brewster Caldwell for every word of encouragement, suggested improvement, and, of course, for their own vital contributions to *Come Shining*. This book is truly a team effort.

Finally, we would like to recognize every contributor who took the time to entrust us with their favorite poem, memory, or handwritten note. Thank you all for being an integral part of *Come Shining* and the future of Copper Canyon Press.

For our literary ancestors
and those who carry their work forward

But they could sit you down
and tell you how poems are born in silence
and sometimes, in moments of great noise,
of how they arrive like the rain,
unexpectedly cracking open the sky.

Tishani Doshi, from
"Find the Poets"

Contents

PERSONAL VOLTAS

HOW POEMS MOVE

STORIES FROM OUR HOUSE

POEMS FOR TOMORROW

THE LASTING LYRIC

Preface

Bear me along your light-bearing paths. Come shining.

C.D. Wright

Dear Reader,

Yesterday, a friend asked me, "What new are you reading?" It's a simple yet familiar question among book lovers and writer friends, but it's also a question that is deeply at the heart of why anyone writes or publishes or sells books. When considering the fiftieth anniversary of Copper Canyon Press, I wanted to document the Press through its poems and its people, rather than trying to establish a personal canon, and so I turned to a variation of that question. I asked poets, staff, freelancers, board members, interns, and others intimately familiar with the Press to share with me their favorite Copper Canyon poems, along with the stories that make those poems meaningful for them. As *A House Called Tomorrow* began to take shape, the volume of recommendations surprised me: nearly two hundred community members rushed to contribute—they shared stories ranging from a parent's devastating recounting of the loss of a child to an intern's exhilarating description of the first time he held the new poetry manuscript by his literary hero, Ursula K. Le Guin. Although I decided that poetry had to be foremost in our consideration for *A House Called Tomorrow*, I deeply regretted that we didn't have the space to include the personal stories that had accompanied their poem choices—stories of celebration, contemplation, and serendipitous connection. And so *Come Shining* was conceived. It's only fitting that the story of Copper Canyon cannot be contained in one collection.

Every book editor lives that same question—"What new are you reading?"— every time they enter a manuscript. At that moment, an editor engages the promise that the writer will offer a fresh view of the familiar, or a reminder that there's so much unfamiliar yet to be found in any individual life. Personally, when I'm in the intimate space of a book, silently in communion with the author, I'm simultaneously thinking of some other potential reader, about a colleague or friend who might like the book I'm holding. And I'm thinking about some beloved unknown reader who might find delight and wisdom in that book. Although a book begins and ends in the parallel solitude of a writer and a reader, it becomes communal when we share it with others, who in turn further enliven the conversation. My colleagues at the Press presumably share this same desire for discovery and book advocacy. My coeditor for this anthology, Kaci X. Tavares, along with Copper Canyon's other editors, expresses a desire to transform her interior engagement with a poem or a book into an exterior enthusiasm. And it's not just editors who do this: during every staff meeting we open and close with a poem, taking turns to point out something we're each excited about. We want to talk about poems, to share the undeniable thrill in finding something new, even in an old book. Through publishing, the solitudinous acts of reading and writing become communal.

Yet rarely does one ask, "What *old* are you reading?" I suspect that this question comes with a more threatening suggestion of vulnerable inadequacy, that the tired old notions of canon-making might create a fear of being judged for one's answer. Or, perhaps, it's too intimate a question, asking the reader to stray beyond current fashion. Yet, this question too is at the heart of *Come Shining*. All the books that have been published by Copper Canyon Press over the past fifty years have in turn made new books possible through the legacy they extend, as well as through you, our dear reader, who adds to our community. Through reading, and through the lens of our community's stories, these poems can be made new again.

In his (re-subtitled) classic, *The Gift: How the Creative Spirit Transforms the World*, Lewis Hyde encourages artists to become "good ancestors" as they pursue their work. Being a good ancestor forwards the creation, intellection, and imagination of those upon whose work new art is built. Antithetically, the American experiment has enshrined individuality and authenticity as paramount in most aspects of contemporary culture, so when an artist, writer, musician, or dancer is deemed to be "gifted," the term often perpetuates the myth of talent arriving sui generis. While those who revivify the ordinary sometimes leave us wondering where their genius comes from, I believe that artists of all stripes—literary, performative, and plastic—continue the work of human expression in relation to *others,* their newness arising in relationship to the old, even—perhaps especially—when mining the material of the self. While there are certainly gifted artists who amaze us in so many unexpected ways with their originality and ability to make the world anew, gifts become gifts when they are given. Whereas the gathering of poems in *A House Called Tomorrow* is akin to the gift of someone reciting a poem—a gift that focuses entirely on poetry—the stories and additional poems you will encounter in *Come Shining* are, as its title suggests, an invitation to participate in the exchange of the gifts of time, attention, and imagination that you bring as a reader.

Another friend, who often stays at my house when I am traveling, regularly leaves behind wonderful books for me upon my return. Coming home, I readily return to the familiar, but through the gift of books left quietly behind, that homecoming now involves transformation and the hungry expectation that I'm returning to something unfamiliar among the familiar. Similarly, in the course of compiling *A House Called Tomorrow,* as I reread suggestions for poems that were already familiar to me, suddenly they were remade by the stories of other readers. Our hope, in turn, is that you, gentle reader, will find transformation in the familiar moments of these pages, that you will find community among poets as well as your fellow poetry admirers.

At Copper Canyon Press, we're more than happy to tell you what we are reading: that's our job as publishers. With *A House Called Tomorrow* and *Come Shining*, I sought to turn the tables somewhat, to honor you, the reader, alongside the writer. These anthologies are an opportunity to attempt good ancestry, to celebrate the communal act of reading, to acknowledge the "public" in publishing. In the following pages you will find, with one exception, poems that weren't included in *A House Called Tomorrow*, largely because the author already was being represented by other recommended work. You will find stories from the many people behind the scenes—people such as our distribution colleagues at Consortium, our dedicated Board of Directors, and our many interns over the years—who have helped us thrive for five decades. You will also find beautifully personal stories and anecdotes about particular poems both in this anthology and its predecessor.

When Copper Canyon Press publishes a book, it is encouraging the promise of future poems by poets who will improve upon the present literary moment. Each book is a grain adding to the lower mountain in the hourglass that turns over in moments of ongoing social and cultural change. The poet has been gifted a constantly shifting palette of languages and dictionaries, and transforms this gift into the next poem upon which a reader may provide voice and transformation. Whenever a poetry reader considers a Copper Canyon Press book, my hope is that they will be surprised and assured in equal measure, that they will begin to understand that that book arises from an intentionally diverse and increasingly varied mix of imaginations and intellects, of life experiences and literary ancestry, of the accessible and the challenging, made new by readers and writers alike.

Dear reader, through the gifts of your time and attention alongside the stories and poems you make possible, you are enlarging the gift and perpetuating generosity. By being a part of a community, you are becoming a good ancestor. Thank you for helping us make Copper Canyon Press what it is and what it will become.

MICHAEL WIEGERS

About the Cover Art

Ut pictura poesis.

Horace

Erika Blumenfeld is a multidisciplinary artist who is the current artist in residence at the National Aeronautics and Space Administration (NASA). Erika was first introduced to us by friends at Lannan Foundation, and Copper Canyon Press has in turn introduced her work to poets whose book covers feature her art. As we were considering ideas for the cover of this anthology, I recalled visiting her studio several years ago, where she showed me and the poet Lisa Olstein her stunning project *Encyclopedia of Trajectories,* which charts and translates meteors into hand-drawn flashes of gold, one of the precious metals brought to earth via meteor strikes during the earth's formation. Blumenfeld first studies NASA recordings of meteors entering our atmosphere and then humanizes those celestial events by using a traditional ink brush to "perform" a single stroke of 24-karat gold onto paper. To quote her project description:

> The *Encyclopedia of Trajectories* project is a quest to activate the long-held knowledge, both scientific and cultural, that we are deeply connected to the universe across its 13.8 billion years. The material composing our bodies shares cosmic origins with the material composing the planets, asteroids and comets in our solar system. Scientifically, this material, having derived from distant stars across time, threads back to the primordial material that emerged moments after our universe burst into being. Culturally, our star gazing has filled us with wonder across all civilizations, sparking art and architecture, philosophy and science, mythology, folklore as well as navigation and place-making. The *Encyclopedia of Trajectories* project intends to study the notion of an embodied relationship with the stars and began with an inquiry into how, in our human form, we can comprehend the immensity of our cosmic heritage—that we are, in our very chemistry, of and from the stars.
>
> To investigate this embodied relationship, I've been drawing every shooting star that occurred over a one-year period. Shooting stars evoke both the wonder of the cosmos and also our longing to have a connection with it, evidenced by the fact that we have, since at least the time of Ptolemy, sent our deepest wishes to them in hopes they might hear us.

The "meteor events" that Blumenfeld studies write their own unique patterns in the darkness—creating bursts of light and motion akin to the poems we are celebrating during our golden anniversary. Poems and entire mythologies have been drawn from the stars, just as Blumenfeld translates the night sky's ineffable moments into single gestures, drawn into a grand community of stars and constellations.

COME SHINING

November 21, 2022

The Copper Canyon poem I chose is by a poet of whom Jim Harrison first made me aware. "Joseph Stroud," Jim said. "His poems remind me of yours, and I'm stunned that I hadn't known of them before." And the Stroud poem which has brought me to write this is called "Provenance," a great meditation seeking a way through grief while wandering a great city, searching through great art and observing the lives of ordinary people, to find consolation for a suffering that cannot be escaped and must finally be embraced.

I return to this poem when I need it. And _need_ is the word that brings me back to Stroud's poems.

Dan Gerber

When I forget to weep,
I hear the peeping tree toads
creeping up the bark.
— Ruth Stone, "Mantra"

Sam Hamill taught me how to set type with this poem on the old press at Fort Worden. A small mistake in the colophon of the first run necessitated a second, and I ended up with a few free broadsides. I gave one to my mother, one to my father, and kept one for myself. As a result, it's become a family mantra. I love the assonance of these lines, imagining those little tree toads, as we are caught together in Love's golden net.

On "Poem for My Love" by June Jordan

In the same way we don't forget our first love, I haven't forgotten my first love poem. "Poem for My Love" was the earliest poem that made me gasp, the first poem that I copied onto a piece of cardstock and gave to someone, the first one I memorized and recited to a partner. Each time I read it, the feeling comes back.

NATASHA RAO, APR/Honickman First Book Prize winner

On "The mosquito brings you blood, it" by Marianne Boruch

I first read *The Book of Hours* back when I was working as an intern at Copper Canyon, and this poem has stuck with me for the decade since then. There's something about the sense of sudden awareness of your own blood, your own body, and of that awareness being a gift even if it doesn't easily feel like one in the moment. That, I've always found striking.

KATE MORLEY, Intern

On "Curtains" by Ruth Stone

That last line. "See what you miss by being dead." Unforgettable. I have begun to think of poems as memorable or not so memorable. Many good poems are good, but I don't remember them after I read them. And then there are the poems I never forget. Where a line or a whole poem just sticks with me. Those are the ones that turn out to matter—at least to me.

ELLEN BASS, Poet

I adore this poem, and I've brought it to conferences where I had to teach a beloved poem. I love all the tensions of opposites. Its vulnerability. Its tenderness. I might even have it memorized.

TRACI BRIMHALL, Poet

I Could Touch It
Ellen Bass
Indigo (2020)

When she was breaking apart, our son was falling in love.

She lay on the couch with a heated sack of rice on her belly,
sometimes dozing, sometimes staring out the window at the olive tree

as it broke into tiny white blossoms, as it swelled into bitter black fruit.

At first, I wanted to spare him.
I wished he was still farming up north, tucking bulbs of green onions
into their beds and watering the lettuce,
his hands gritty, his head haloed in a straw hat.

But as the months deepened, I grew selfish.

I wanted him here with his new love.
When I passed the open bathroom door, I wanted
to see them brushing their teeth,

one perched on the toilet lid, one on the side of the tub,
laughing and talking through their foamy mouths,
toothbrushes rattling against their teeth.

As sage gives its scent when you crush it. As stone
is hard. They were happy and I could touch it.

At nineteen, I spent three hours every Monday in a seminar—Poetry Can Save Your Life—led by Greg Orr. Nearly every week, I'd sit in his office for thirty minutes after class talking about how to live a life: how he lived his, how poetry was vital to it, and how I might live mine. I set my phone to record every conversation; I now have hours and hours of voice memos with us talking about everything from Dylan Thomas's alcoholism to Sappho's love poetry to the nights that Keats kept him company in an Alabama jail cell.

   At the time, I had no clue what I was doing in practically any area of my life, but I knew I needed to be sitting in that little third-floor office just as often as Greg would allow me in. I turned twenty that year and lived perpetually standing inside myself "like a dead tree," or worse. Greg's poetry and kindness gave me the tools and language to pull myself out of myself, to reawaken to the world and to longing. Years later, many months sober and alone on a road trip in the western US to hug some (living) trees, I found myself standing in an open field, midhike, waiting for the rain clouds hanging overhead to burst. When they did, I was so grateful to be so full of love I wept.

JAY BAKER, Intern

Self-Portrait at Twenty

Gregory Orr
The Caged Owl: New and Selected Poems (2002)

I stood inside myself
like a dead tree or a tower.
I pulled the rope
of braided hair
and high above me
a bell of leaves tolled.

Because my hand
stabbed its brother,
I said: Make it stone.

Because my tongue
spoke harshly, I said:
Make it dust.
                And yet
it was not death, but
her body in its green dress
I longed for. That's why
I stood for days in the field
until the grass turned black
and the rain came.

How Beautiful the Beloved remains my favorite Copper Canyon Press book of their many published books and poets. Within it, there are so many strong poems. I admire his brevity and power in the right words chosen.

> Poem that opened you—
> The opposite of a wound.
>
> Didn't the world
> Come pouring through?

JOAN M. BROUGHTON, Financial Consultant

Loss and loss and more

Gregory Orr
How Beautiful the Beloved (2009)

Loss and loss and more
Loss—that's what
The sea teaches.

The need to stay
Nimble
Against the suck
Of receding waves,
The sand
Disappearing
Under our feet.

Here, where sea
Meets shore:
The best of dancing floors.

I return to Nicholas Goodly's "First Poem" again and again for its radiant sweetness and kaleidoscopic remembering. Here, recollection is an imaginative process, memory swirling into memory, the soil rich with poetic possibility. And how could a poet have only one origin, Goodly asks, when every recollection plants another seed? Here is their second first poem, a new bloom in the good(ly) garden.

ELIZABETH BRUEGGEMANN, Intern

First Poem
Nicholas Goodly
Black Swim (2022)

I had ever written was about green bug
because I painted one at school or the painting
came later to go with the poem or the poem
was about gold and was printed in rainbow letters
and the painting had a rainbow in it the picture
was a blue watering bucket a butterfly an orange-
and-pink sunset made of vertical stripes
and a purple rainbow and a rose or tulip
and the poem had a refrain it was a song
a song for class or I wrote it for my dance
teacher because she thought I was a poet
and I read it to the class or just to her she said
beautiful or thank you and the painting and poem
are in a frame together now and it matters
that where it all started was a good garden

On "Gizzard Song" by Dean Young

My friend Wif, aged fifty, had a heart transplant, and has been struggling for over a year with rejection issues. I learned today that he may need a second transplant. That brought me back to "Gizzard Song" by Dean Young, a poem I shared with Wif at the time of his first transplant. It brought Dean's humor, compassion, and shared experience to Wif—a light moment, during a deadly serious time. Light and transcendent, a very poetic combination.

WALTER PARSONS, Board Member

On "Provenance" by Joseph Stroud

I think Joe's poem "Provenance" is one of the purest, most beautiful, most emotionally intelligent and spiritually meaningful portraits of grief I've ever read. It's astonishing. I carry that poem with me every day.

ERIN BELIEU, Poet

On "Daddy Longlegs" by Ted Kooser

Ted Kooser's "Daddy Longlegs" may seem like an unusual choice, but it has lingered in my brain for years. I have a spider phobia—full-blown shaking, heart-racing, "Where do I run?" type of phobia. But my mom, who passed away at fifty-seven, always calmed me as a child if the spider was a daddy longlegs. "They are our friends because they eat mosquitoes." Living in Minnesota, that made a convincing argument. But they are also elegant and fragile creatures. They don't skittle across surfaces as a menacing hairy blur. They are to be admired. If I see one, I'm not afraid, but inspired to walk "alone across the floor of my life / with an easy grace," like my friend.

JANNA RADEMACHER, Consortium Book Sales & Distribution Client Relations Manager

August Zero was the first book of Jane Miller's I ever read and it blew my mind, this poem especially. I still remember where I found it—in a bookstore that's also a mill in Massachusetts. I brought the books I'd chosen up to the register and the woman working there told me I had chosen a lot of James Tate's books, which had recently been donated to the store. There are pencil marks and underlines in my copy; it's something I hold very dear.

CHESSY NORMILE, APR/Honickman
First Book Prize winner

August Zero

Jane Miller
August Zero (1993)

Young trees the bright green of a moonless night,
lawn the red of scorpion,—

the pleasure dome drops, a drill ceases and a mower resumes.
It hides the spectacle of the mountains
and jolts us, it's been a long time
since we've had a little space to ourselves.

All the same, in spite of everything,
we are made to live in the air, which involves a certain number
of mental operations
the full force of a bow, a revision of the notion
of history,
oddly imitating the movements of animals when I think about it,
doubling back, appearing to be shot or struck—

and celestial sounds, not sound itself
rock the bare earth, packed hard and nailed
to the tune of the unconscious,
which we regret to understand.

Don't get me wrong, there's still a knowledge of freedom,
a bath, a change of clothing,
possession of a child's heart,
a handshake, and the function of time
a detail—even in air
language is a
cross between an appetite and a mouth—

I'm not hungry when I'm lonely.
Like all the lead and neon which is forgotten
I forget that people have died forever,
no one knows you
and the ideal place is a dome with horses' shadows
the shade of steel gin,
and what formerly acceded to a view constitutes love.

A pear—
remember now future became present—
in a kitchen and two rooms in orbit
pins the horizon with its pony body and elk head
and we enact where we first made love the camellia of our beloved—
we can't touch exactly
but attempt a profound correlation—
we grip the skeleton of a river and the sun kisses it
like one's own throat.

This is the earth, my love, all of us
have a chunk on our backs.
You are an angel
and I am an ancient
who're cast from two and a half billion cars a day

into one copter night,
and closure is that windmill
through a wall in the circle, drifting
like the once innocent

oil spills in the Pacific,
like conversation.

I find solace in this poem every time I am in despair or, more often, in drunkenness.

May You Always Be the Darling of Fortune

Jane Miller
Memory at These Speeds: New & Selected Poems (1996)

March 10th and the snow flees like eloping brides
into rain. The imperceptible change begins
out of an old rage and glistens, chaste, with its new
craving, spring. May your desire always overcome

your need; your story that you have to tell,
enchanting, mutable, may it fill the world
you believe: a sunny view, flowers lunging
from the sill, the quilt, the chair, all things

fill with you and empty and fill. And hurry because
now as I tire of my studied abandon, counting
the days, I'm sad. Yet I trust your absence, in everything
wholly evident: the rain in the white basin and I

vigilant.

Isadora
Robert Hedin
Snow Country (1975)

> *quotations from* The Art of the Dance
> *by Isadora Duncan*

Kyrie kyrie say yes to Isadora
Say yes say yes to madame Dolorosa
Say yes to Walt Whitman yes to Yesenin
Say yes say yes kyrie kyrie

"Often when people have questioned my morals, I have answered that I
consider myself extremely moral because in all my relations I have only made
movements which seem beautiful to me."

Tonight Isadora beauty is home
And if beauty is home then I sleep
I send my arms deep into its darkness
Tracing along its cool wet paths
Through fogs that rise and swirl
Curling like your scarves past my hands
Because Isadora beauty is home
And if beauty is home then I sleep
And moving deeper I see you rise
Stand and dance your scarves
You let your body shine pale
Because Isadora tonight beauty is home
And if beauty is home then I sleep
I feel the sweep of your gown
I breathe with your hair
I ride the currents of your lungs
I swim with your hands
Because Isadora beauty is your home
And if beauty is your home then I sleep

"Of all movement which gives us delight and satisfies the soul's sense of
movement, that of the waves of the sea seems to me the finest. This great
wave movement runs through all Nature."

And tonight Isadora the waves run long
I feel their inner lifts and falls
And in turn receive your dance your loves

And I name you Whitman my Yesenin
And say yes because Isadora the waves run long
I watch your white arabesque
Crest with each live swell
I watch your scarves move out across the sand
I watch your pulse drive and dance over the rocks
And I hear the dark cup your purple flecks of light
And the tide running long says

Kyrie kyrie say yes to Isadora
Say yes say yes to madame Dolorosa
Say yes to Walt Whitman yes to Yesenin
Say yes say yes kyrie kyrie

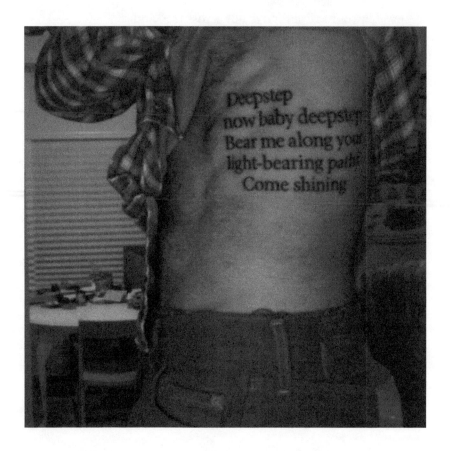

Copper Canyon Press copyeditor and proofreader David Caligiuri has on occasion added texts to his body. A longtime friend of C.D. Wright, David added this quote on his ribs to honor the poet after her death. Set in 51-point type to recognize his fifty-first year, the quote is reversed so as to be read in a mirror. It is set (by Valerie Brewster Caldwell, who resized the periods for balance, codesigning the tattoo) in Minion type because C.D. once joked with him that "we're all minions in poetry."

Deepstep Come Shining may be C.D. Wright's finest poem.

ARTHUR SZE, Poet and Translator

from *Deepstep Come Shining*

C.D. Wright
Deepstep Come Shining (1998)

Pattycake lives here. She's one of the Jumping Foxes, the Double-Dutch Champs. Can you take her picture while we're here. I'll look for the funeral of a stranger to attend.

He's not rambling is he.

The end of the silver queen. I've got to have me one more cob before I croak.

Odontokeratoprosthesis: a tooth for an eye. A gruesome procedure, but not a bad trade.

The donor of course must not have syphilis. Why don't you call back after the 4th.

At one time Milledgeville was a bird sanctuary.

The worst is not so long as we can say, "This is the worst." Isn't that the truth. Deepstep now baby deepstep. Bear me along your light-bearing paths. Come shining.

I'm not long on ruins, but I wanted to stop. The walls of the church were intact. The chairs and pews were wrecked. But the baptismal font, with seven descending steps, I had never seen one emptied out. Trumpet vine in profusion over every brick and windowpane.

Mystery, mystery and a curse.

The watery grave. Take the boneman's hand.

Is that your cane slashing through the grass.

Deepstep come shining.

If I shell those beans for you, will you cook a mess for me. There goes Hannah behind that cloudlet.

They hung in there when I was broke and sorry.
They hung in there when I was mean and nasty.
They hung in there when I was drunk and strung out.
They hung on in.

#4.
I keep coming back to the closing passage in C.D.
Wright's Deepstep Come Shining, where the speaker says,

"In the hither world I lead you willingly along the light-
bearing paths. In the hither world, I offer a once-and-for-all
thing"...

I remember the day we drove around Rhode Island and looked at
beech trees in cemeteries. The day was not mournful but instead
filled with streaming light. C.D.'s words continue to help
light the way.   — Lee Sye

I've carried these lines—"I am trying to invent a new way of moving under my / dress: the room squares off against this"—around with me for the last twenty years. Wright's words remain the perfect summation of how I felt as a restless girl in an immigrant family just trying to assimilate. How I feel today as a female writer at odds with an American culture that would prefer my silence. I savor the presence of the physical body here, sensual and splendid. And I treasure this poem as a reminder that while "seizing happi / ness" is my right, it's also enough just to be here.

ANGELA GARBES, Publicist and Intern

Crescent
C.D. Wright
Steal Away (2002)

In recent months I have become intent on seizing happi-
ness: to this end I applied various shades of blue: only
the evening is outside us now propagating honeysuckle:
I am trying to invent a new way of moving under my
dress: the room squares off against this: watch the water
glitter with excitement: when we cut below the silver
skin of the surface the center retains its fluidity: do I still
remind you of a locust clinging to a branch: I give you
an idea of the damages: you would let edges be edges:
believe me: when their eyes poured over your long body
of poetry I also was there: when they laid their hands on
your glass shade I also was there: when they put their
whole trust in your grace I had to step outside to get
away from my cravenness: we have done these things to
each other without benefit of a mirror: unlike the hon-
eysuckle goodness does not overtake us: yet the thigh
keeps quiet under nylon: later beneath the blueness of
trees the future falls out of place: something always hap-
pens: draw nearer my dear: never fear: the world spins
nightly toward its brightness and we are on it

On "Slow Song for Mark Rothko" by John Taggart

It was through C.D. Wright that I discovered the work of John Taggart. I was already a devoted reader of C.D.'s work, which was good enough reason for me to be curious about Taggart on her recommendation. "Slow Song for Mark Rothko" never fails me, and I have read it often, usually out loud. It is just not like anything else. It is extraordinary.

ALISON LOCKHART, Copyeditor, Proofreader, and Intern

On "Elegy for Ted Berrigan" by Stephen Kuusisto

Although the form of "Elegy for Ted Berrigan" is simple and highly crafted, the territory it covers as speaker-poet, reader, and person is immense and beautiful for its honesty. In my twenties, I heard Stephen read it at the Port Townsend Writers Conference. It spoke to me clearly, and since then, I have lived with the last sentence—it visits me often.

NELLIE BRIDGE, Letterpress Printer and Intern

On "Antenna-Forest" by Rolf Jacobsen, translated from the Norwegian by Robert Hedin

Jacobsen is one of my absolute all-time favorite poets, but maybe here he stands in for all the poets I didn't know or didn't know well enough until I read them in Copper Canyon Press translations. This poem is so easy and charming, but almost every line is a huge reimagining."

JAMES RICHARDSON, Poet

On "Drunk Monsoon" by Alberto Ríos

I've always been a bit obsessed with poems about rain: the kind that mists, the kind that cries, the kind that makes you want to tilt your head back and drink it. "Drunk Monsoon" by Alberto Ríos captures such a deluge, while revealing a timely exhaustion and desire to connect that we hold in all of us. This poem will always stay with me, as I got to open one of my first Copper Canyon staff meetings with it, surrounded by those who believe just as much as I do in poetry's power to uplift.

KACI X. TAVARES, Development Manager, Publishing Fellow, and Intern

On "Hovering" by Joseph Stroud

This gorgeous, short poem perfectly encapsulates our relationship with time and nature, and celebrates time spent with friends. My taste generally skews more experimental, but this poem slays me every time I read it.

PHIL KOVACEVICH, Book and Pressmark Designer

On "Ezra Under the Constellation of the Dragon" by Joseph Stroud

This poem and Joe's "The First Law of Thermodynamics" remain vital to me. The "Ezra" poem is in dialogue with Canto LXXXI, of course, another piece close to my heart: *"Master thyself, then others shall thee beare"*—such comedy that I could weep.

DAVID CALIGIURI, Copyeditor and Proofreader

The last four lines of "As a Human Being" haunt me, especially "finally / Free now that nobody's got to love you." I've never been able to articulate this feeling for myself the way Jericho does in this very last line. The ecstasy and agony of being loved. The ecstasy and agony of being unloved. To be unloved comes with a certain freedom: maybe you can finally grasp the happiness you've always deserved, especially when you've been hurt again and again by the people who purport to love you. But the cost—it's stitched in scar tissue. In the years since I first read this poem, through all that has happened since, Jericho's lingering words are constant companions.

IVY MARIE, Intern

As a Human Being

Jericho Brown
The Tradition (2019)

There is the happiness you have
And the happiness you deserve.
They sit apart from each other
The way you and your mother
Sat on opposite ends of the sofa
After an ambulance came to take
Your father away. Some good
Doctor will stitch him up, and
Soon an aunt will arrive to drive
Your mother to the hospital
Where she will settle next to him
Forever, as promised. She holds
The arm of her seat as if she could
Fall, as if it is the only sturdy thing,
And it is, since you've done what
You always wanted, you fought
Your father and won, marred him.
He'll have a scar he can see all
Because of you. And your mother,
The only woman you ever cried for,
Must tend to it as a bride tends
To her vows, forsaking all others
No matter how sore the injury.
No matter how sore the injury
Has left you, you sit understanding
Yourself as a human being finally
Free now that nobody's got to love you.

I can relate.

JOSH BROWN, Consortium Book
Sales & Distribution Operations and
Metadata Supervisor

Theory of Aging

Ursula K. Le Guin
So Far So Good: Final Poems: 2014–2018 (2018)

As the number of the year gets bigger
the year itself grows smaller
but heavier. It acquires gravity.
It will finally get so heavy
that it cannot continue as it is
but implodes to a black hole
into which sink all the years
becoming numberless
and utterly weightless.

This is a longtime favorite of mine. I refer to it continuously for inspiration and contemplation.

CATHERINE EDWARDS, Board Member

Priceless Gifts

Anna Swir, translated from the Polish
by Czesław Miłosz and Leonard Nathan
Talking to My Body (1996)

An empty day without events.
And that is why
it grew immense
as space. And suddenly
happiness of being
entered me.

I heard
in my heartbeat
the birth of time
and each instant of life
one after the other
came rushing in
like priceless gifts.

"A Spiral Notebook" is one of the wonders of the world. It ranks right up there with the No. 2 pencil. Essential to this life, it speaks to hope, potential, and imagination. A blue spiral notebook: simple yet astonishing. And every bit as indispensable and necessary as the poems of Ted Kooser.

RICHARD JONES, Poet

A Spiral Notebook

Ted Kooser
Delights & Shadows (2004)

The bright wire rolls like a porpoise
in and out of the calm blue sea
of the cover, or perhaps like a sleeper
twisting in and out of his dreams,
for it could hold a record of dreams
if you wanted to buy it for that,
though it seems to be meant for
more serious work, with its
college-ruled lines and its cover
that states in emphatic white letters,
5 SUBJECT NOTEBOOK. It seems
a part of growing old is no longer
to have five subjects, each
demanding an equal share of attention,
set apart by brown cardboard dividers,
but instead to stand in a drugstore
and hang on to one subject
a little too long, like this notebook
you weigh in your hands, passing
your fingers over its surfaces
as if it were some kind of wonder.

On "Swinging from Parents" by Ted Kooser

I remember my first time reading "Swinging from Parents," how I latched on to the use of words and letters as image: "She makes the shape of the *y* / at the end of *infancy*, and lifts her feet / the way the *y* pulls up its feet, and swings." This kind of wordplay was new for me, fascinating.

Now when I call home, my grandmother has forgotten her teeth on the bathroom counter and my mother complains of her knees, how they've swollen from working too hard—she can't bleach the concrete floors in the washroom anymore, or stay on her feet to cook Sunday dinner. She says she needs help. Lately, I've been thinking about death.

I return to this poem again and again, hanging on the word *forever*. I shudder at Kooser's brilliant use of tension: what the child knows versus what the reader knows. Forever is no place for trust. I return and feel the longing and mortality in each line. "Swinging from Parents" is timeless, universal, changing as you do.

ASHLEY E. WYNTER, Editor

On "No More Cake Here" by Natalie Diaz

"No More Cake Here" was the first of Diaz's poems to get under my skin and stay there—the first of many. The visionary exactness and implausible inevitability of the poem combine a highly crafted lyric style with a sprawling narrative, which, when connected to the rest of the poems in *When My Brother Was an Aztec*, felt like a step forward in what poetry can do. It's a Felliniesque poem of comedy and tragedy, and it always breaks my heart to read it.

ED SKOOG, Poet

A great example of Perillo's voice and intelligence. I never tire of reading this poem.

JOHN PIERCE, Managing Editor

Samara

Lucia Perillo
On the Spectrum of Possible Deaths (2012)

1.

At first they're yellow butterflies
whirling outside the window—

but no: they're flying seeds.
An offering from the maple tree,

hard to believe the earth-engine capable of such invention,
that the process of mutation and dispersal
will not only formulate the right equations

but that when they finally arrive they'll be so
. . . *giddy?*

2.

Somewhere Darwin speculates that happiness
should be the outcome of his theory—

those who take pleasure
will produce offspring who'll take pleasure,

though he concedes the advantage of the animal who keeps death in mind
and so is vigilant.

And doesn't vigilance call for
at least an ounce of expectation,
imagining the lion's tooth inside your neck already,

for you to have your best chance of outrunning the lion

on the arrival of the lion.

3.

When it comes time to "dedicate the merit"
the Buddhists chant *from the ocean of samsara*
may I free all beings—

at first I misremembered, and thought
the word for the seed the same.

Meaning "the wheel of birth and misery and death,"
nothing in between the birth and death but misery,

surely an overzealous bit of whittlework
on the part of *Webster's Third New International Unabridged*

(though if you eliminate dogs and pie and swimming
feels about right to me—

oh shut up, Lucia. The rule is: you can't nullify the world
in the middle of your singing).

4.

In the Autonomous Vehicle Laboratory
RoboSeed is flying.
It is not a sorrow though its motor makes an annoying sound.

The doctoral students have calculated
the correct thrust-to-weight ratio and heave dynamics.
On YouTube you can watch it flying in the moonlight
outside the engineering building with the fake Ionic columns.

I said "sorrow" for the fear that in the future all the beauties
will be replaced by replicas that have more glare and blare and bling.
RoboSeed, RoboRose, RoboHeart, RoboSoul—

this way there'll be no blight
on any of the cherished encapsulations

when the blight was what we loved.

5.

They grow in chains from the bigleaf maple, chains
that lengthen until they break.
In June,

when the days are long and the sky is full
and the swept pile thickens
with the ones grown brown and brittle—

oh see how I've underestimated the persistence
of the lace in their one wing.

6.

Is there no slim chance I will feel it

when some molecule of me
(annealed by fire, like coal or glass)

is drawn up in the phloem of a maple
(please scatter my ashes under a maple)

so my speck can blip out
on a stem sprouting out of the fork of a branch,

the afterthought of a flower
that was the afterthought of a bud,

transformed now into a seed with a wing,
like the one I wore on the tip of my nose

back when I was green.

When I think of the many outstanding poems that might represent Copper Canyon Press, one of the first that comes to mind is Sam Hamill's "Reading Seferis." This poem beautifully, heartbreakingly reimagines the Hellenistic "acceptance of life," a complex set of perceptions and values that became, over the couple of years leading up to the founding of Copper Canyon Press, a foundational element of the editorial aesthetic of the Press.

WILLIAM O'DALY, Press Cofounder, Poet, and Translator

Reading Seferis
Sam Hamill
Animae (1980)

to Olga Broumas

"Not many moonlit nights
have given me pleasure."
The stars spell out
the ancient mathematics
of the heart in huge
desolate zeros, ciphers
of nothing, and despite it all,
I care. There is a fatigue
in the crumbling of cities
for which there is no cure,
no penance or catharsis,
not even a prayer—only
the will to endure. The heavy
torpor of gray-brown air,
the lethargy of the soul—
by these we measure out
each crisis, each ancient debt
we don't repay the poor.

There are not many moons
I remember. The Sound
is blue where it reflects
the dark sky of night
or the bright sky of day.
Amica silentia lunae,
and each day the sun
drowns in fire and water—

a metaphor for nothing,
the unaccountable longing.
Some would call upon the moon
for power, for pure sexual
pleasure, but that is unholy
and denies both the sowing
and the reaping. The moon
is not a scythe that mows
the tall mute grass of heaven.

But we, Olga, are grasses
wavering in breezes
of politics and dollars, we
are the exiles of the earth,
the rooted and swarthy
who see the moon in everything
and think it a symbol
for our suffering. It is
the human mind that curves
into a razor, that harvests
human pain. We shall be
the chaff which flies
in the cutting, the lullaby
of the fields that is not heard
on moonless nights because
only moonlight is romantic.

I hear the lullaby of victims
who are happy. Few are the moons
for them, and even these
are imagined. I imagine the full
moon of a smile, the moon
of my buttocks when I was a boy
and a prankster, the twin
moons of my lover's breasts,
the stars, oh, in her eyes
and I love her. Olga,
these are the maps, topographies
of the heart that tell us
everything: we are all
the victims, we are heroes also
and slaves. Seferis says
the heroes are the ones
move forward in the dark.

I remember the terrible
darkness of my childhood
and the fear. And the moon
was more fearsome, more awe-full
with its wails and howls
and its shadows. I remember
the moon as female, Loba, yesterday
when she raged. I tire so soon
of metaphor! I want to send you,
Olga, the alphabet of stars
which ask for nothing
and offer a little light
against the dark we wear;
I want to offer the warmth
of a lullaby, the kiss of deep
sleep, a reflection of the moon
reflected on the waters
of your song—so few
are the moonlit nights
that I've cared for.

                    full moon
                    VIII:40079

On "Birds Hover the Trampled Field" by Richard Siken

I am not sure how to talk about Richard Siken's "Birds Hover the Trampled Field" without getting into all the specifics of what each line means to me, and that would turn into a therapy session. That's the power of this poem and how I find myself turning to it each time I find myself in ruin. The very premise of the poem is found in the following lines: "I wanted to explain / myself to myself in an understandable way." In this poem, Siken exposes just how difficult it is to be honest with oneself.

ZUHRA AMINI, Intern

On "Anagrammer" by Peter Pereira

Peter Pereira's "Anagrammer" brought back the joy and playfulness in poetry for me—it is smart and funny, but also thoughtful. It is still a poem I can read again and again, and yes, it inspired my own anagram poems.

KELLI RUSSELL AGODON, Poet

On "Something Is Dying Here" by Thomas McGrath

Lines from Thomas McGrath's "Something Is Dying Here" come to my mind often. I also have a broadside of it on my wall. This poem encapsulates Thomas McGrath's energy, I think, that of the Midwest and a slight overcast hopelessness that pervades rural life.

COLE W. WILLIAMS, Intern

I don't think we ever get over our parents' deaths; some days it's easier, and other days, harder. When Carruth writes, "Oh how he lay there / quiet as cast dice, crooked," I know exactly what he means. The grief detailed in "My Father's Face"—confused, nonspecific, full of rage—tides me over when it seems, even over a decade later, that my own father's death will never properly submerge. "What am I now, // what is my sorrow, has it not spun away?"

NOAH LLOYD, Intern

My Father's Face
Hayden Carruth
Collected Longer Poems (1993)

Old he was but not yet wax,
old and old but not yet gray.
What an awkwardness of facts
gray and waxen when he lay.

Rage had held me forty years,
only five have sought his grace.
Will my disproportionate tears
quell at last his smiling face?

Awkwardly at his behest
I this queer rhyme try to make
after one that he loved best,
made long since by Willy Blake.

~

Cannot. In
my own way, half inarticulate,
must sing the blues.

Oh how he lay there
quiet as cast dice, crooked. They had given him
a face he never wore

smiling like anyone,
like God—
he, my own, who had smiled only

in the smear of pain,
as now my hemlock smears in this wind
dripping with half-snow, half-rain.

Smoke flares from my stovepipe,
breaks sharply down, away,
blue, whipping the leafless alders, vanishing,

while I watch from my window, this shack
in a scrap of meadow
going to woods—

alder, chokecherry, yellow birch, ash,
and the one old hemlock leaning forth,
smeared in half-snow, half-rain, November and the north.

~

Southward, downcountry
was where he lay
and I stood

in a loathsome mass of bleeding flowers
that April. Sun flashed and was gone, cold.
We two there, lashed stiff in old antagonism,

yet altered. It was that new smile
fingered on him, official, patented,
like the oil that shone on the pale oak catafalque:

such means they use to publicize, to promote
a marketable death.
He was worthy, worthy!—

I blurted, tried to blurt
in the clench of a surprise of tears.
And then my anger shifted from him to them.

In that horror
of hurting flowers
where I stood and he lay

I, frozen, was turned around inside my years
as a shadow turns
inside the changing day.

~

Why couldn't they let him be himself?
Like all our family he smiled
with a downturned mouth.

No doubt professional death-tenders are required,
competence is required, yet I wish they had let him
lie as he had fallen,

old Darwinist smiling
at the light gone down in the south,
at the leaf gone down.

Strangely, the birds had come. Already
in cold twilight robins sang,
and he heard them, the simple but rich song,

like Blake's, melodious for a fair season to come,
he heard them and he fell down,
unable to last till summer.

It was a reversal.
At the wrong time, in April, light dwindled
and the leaf fell down.

But hearts burst any time.
He took it smiling
with a downturned mouth.

~

The old Socialist!
And his father before him.
Era of eyeshades, rolltops, late tracks in a snowy street,

a flare of shots maybe in the dark,
and the talk, talk: that man eating,
this man not.

It was all so blessedly simple.
Hate, hate the monopolists!
Ah, and have I not, sirrah?—

but power of money has bought the power of heart,
monopoly eats the word, eats thought, desire,
your old companions now in the thick of it, eating—

is that betrayal? They fatten, but for my part
old hatred deepens,
deepening as monopoly deepens,

until my socialism has driven me to the sociality
of trees, snow, rocks, the north—solitude.
Strange outcome. Like so many.

I'll walk now; the woody meadow,
the firs, the brook, then higher to the birches.
I wish you were coming too.

~

"Alyosha left his father's house
feeling more depressed and
crushed in spirit

than when he entered it . . ." I walk,
going at last nowhere
in the snow and rain

that lock in air
and nap the gray rock with gray fur.
Beside me, among the ferns that confide

their green trust to the snow,
something stalks, or seems to stalk. A partridge?
Or my mind's shadow? Minute fires flow

in the lichened rock, and a yellow eye
blinks like a shuttered lens among the ferns.
Shadows and strange fires,

who can deny them, aspects of the cold world
and the father's house? We rebel
backward, ever backward, going

behind the ancestral impositions of reality.
To seek, to find—not to impose. So we say.
But it is a sad business.

~

Once he brought
to his blue house in the guttering chestnut forest—
oh, I remember this—

a pomegranate in his pocket.
But let me describe to you a killed chestnut tree.
Leaves, fruit, even the bark have long fallen

to the dark alien disease, and at last
the tree itself lies down
in a twisted, rising-and-falling

shape, and it never rots.
The smooth wood, pale and intense,
undulates

in a kind of serpentine passivity
among waves of witch hazel and dogwood
that wash along it

summer after summer after summer.
And so the killed chestnut has become
something everlasting in the woods,

like Yggdrasill. Tradition is not convention.
Tradition is always unexpected,
like the taste of the pomegranate, so sweet.

~

I must complete my turning.
With purpose, very coolly, I raise my vision,
snipping

a thread of the net that holds
everything together.
My splashing fears subside about my knees.

How easy! I wonder why
I took so long, learning
that to destroy

what could never be either right or wrong,
this net, this mere order
or any order,

is no real destruction—
look, I walk as I have always walked,
one foot in front of the other foot.

The rocks and birches take so warmly
to the purity of their restoration. I see this.
I have done it with one gesture, like that.

I walk in the tact of the ultimate rebel
graduated from conspiracy,
free, truly free, in the wonder of uncreation.

~

Well, the traditions of woods are sweet,
but something is withheld, something . . .
O my father, where is the real monopolist?

Can I, alien, avoid spreading
my dark disease? But you would say then,
seek its purity, deep at the root, radically.

If the orderly massacre of order creates an order,
then let it be new, even now, from the beginnings of things.
I am cold to my bones, my red hand clings

like a wind-plastered leaf to a white bole of birch,
the sky is speckled with snow-flecks
driven downwind, vanishing. It is all a song

vanishing down the wind, like snow,
like the last leaves of the birch
spinning away in harsh beauty. The hardhack,

clotted with snow, bends and rattles,
a sound like jeering in the driven twilight.
Why must the song be so intricate? What am I now,

what is my sorrow, has it not spun away?
Your face, snow-flecked, seems torn
downwind like the song of birch leaves.

~

Confused darkness turns a page. Wind slackens,
cold night is beginning, in the last light
the god of winter walks, gray and alone,

Odin, Windigo, Saint Malachy, someone
with a downturned smile brushing the fir boughs,
shaking the dead reeds and ferns.

Snow thickens, leaning toward the south.
Could he come home tonight
to his house, his woods, the snow, the snow-light?

My thought sings into snow, vanishing.
At least I have two clear choices: to stamp
in deepening cold, half-blind, dragging

my feet in freezing ferns, determining
my way in darkness, to the ragged meadow,
the shack with the rusty stove;

or to stay where I am in the rustle of snow
while my beard clots and whitens
and the world recedes into old purity

and the snow opens at last to the stars
that will glisten like silent histories breaking
over a silent face, smiling and cold.

~

O thou quiet northern snow
reaching southward wave on wave,
southward to the land below,
billow gently on his grave.

Snowy owl that glides alone,
softly go, defend his rest;
buntings, whirl around his stone
softly, thou the wintriest.

Gently, softly, o my kind,
snow and wind and driven leaf,
take him, teach my rebel mind
trust at last in this cold grief.

Mantra

Ruth Stone
In the Next Galaxy (2002)

When I am sad
I sing, remembering
the redwing blackbird's clack.
Then I want no thing
except to turn time back
to what I had
before love made me sad.

When I forget to weep,
I hear the peeping tree toads
creeping up the bark.
Love lies asleep
and dreams that everything
is in its golden net;
and I am caught there, too,
when I forget.

Reuben Gelley Newman, 11/23/22
Fall 2020 intern:

I first ordered Night Sky
with Exit Wounds directly
from the press in 2016 and
or 2017, as I was starting to
get serious about poetry. I
scribbled a note on almost
every page — a well-loved book.
A couple years later, I found
a used copy of Library of
Small Catastrophes, another treasured
collection. So grateful!

Published by The Kayrock Screenprinting Corporation.
Brooklyn, New York. www.kayrock.org
No. 5

THIS SIDE FOR CORRESPONDENCE

THIS SIDE FOR ADDRESS ONLY

Copper Canyon Press
NAME
Come Shining Project
PO Box 271
ADDRESS

Port Townsend, WA
98368

In the dream I return
        to the river of bees —
                        W.S. Merwin

I found this poem while feverish in Moscow,
Russia, thirty years ago, and it was like finding
a language for such feverish exile, such
a dream from which I could not wake
nor find the words to explain.
For a ½ century
    of such gifts! — Philip Metres

So many books to choose
from, but Dana Levin's
In The Surgical Theatre
amazed me when I read
it 23 years ago. It changed
my own writing then and
now.
            Kevin Prufer

On "I Am an Ox in the Year of the Horse" by Michael McGriff

In the spring of 2017, I was fortunate enough to have Mike serve on my MFA thesis committee at the University of Idaho. I didn't know him well, but I knew his poems. When *Early Hour* was published in August of 2017, I eagerly devoured the new collection on a rainy afternoon in Olympia. As I finished the final poem, "I Am an Ox in the Year of the Horse," I was stunned, utterly and completely stunned. As Emily Dickinson might say, the top of my head was taken off. I sat there by the window, my body frozen, and I swear to you, the sun parted those thick, dripping clouds and laid its bare hands right on my face—not even that sweltering Leo light could warm me.

JOSH HAMILTON, Intern

On "Barbie Chang's Tears" by Victoria Chang

I remember reading Victoria Chang's *Barbie Chang* while interning at Copper Canyon Press. It was at a time where I was feeling pretty "burned out" from consuming poetry, but that collection had such a unique combination of darkness and whimsicality it helped shake through the haze! I think "Barbie Chang's Tears" embodies what I loved best about the collection—deliberately idiosyncratic, almost a parody of a poem, but still having this dark underbelly that draws you in.

LAUREL LARSON-HARSCH, Intern

On "Postscript" by Dan Gerber

Several years ago, I started signing off on e-mails and messages with "Love." I began to realize that a number of my regular contacts were, in fact, signing off their responses to me with "Love." *Hey, is it catching?* Perhaps. And then I read Dan's beautiful poem "Postscript," and that said it all. I don't want to wish I told more people I loved them when I come to the end of my life. I'd much rather be accused of being too familiar, of sending the wrong signal, as Dan puts it.

BOB FRANCIS, Volunteer

Dan Gerber was one of the first poets I encountered on my own, independent of a teacher guiding me on who and what to read. I was in my early twenties and hitchhiking across the United States, and I decided to visit northern Michigan and the Upper Peninsula. In a rural bookstore I found a gorgeous volume of poems and bought the book rather than eat lunch that day (tight traveling budget). The book was by Dan Gerber, and since that fateful meeting, I've read every book of poems Dan's ever published. I return to "Postscript" often because it reminds me to tell those people I love just that.

JOSEPH BEDNARIK, Copublisher and Marketing Director

The Loon on Forrester's Pond

Hayden Carruth
Collected Shorter Poems, 1946–1991 (1992)

Summer wilderness, a blue light
twinkling in trees and water, but even
wilderness is deprived now. "What's that?
What is that sound?" Then it came to me,
this insane song, wavering music
like the cry of the genie inside the lamp,
it came from inside the long wilderness
of my life, a loon's song, and there he was
swimming on the pond, guarding
his mate's nest by the shore,
diving and staying under
unbelievable minutes and coming up
where no one was looking. My friend
told how once in his boyhood
he had seen a loon swimming beneath his boat,
a shape dark and powerful
down in that silent mysterious world, and how
it had ejected a plume of white excrement
curving behind. "It was beautiful,"
he said.

The loon
broke the stillness over the water
again and again,
broke the wilderness
with his song, truly
a vestige, the laugh that transcends
first all mirth
and then all sorrow
and finally all knowledge, dying
into the gentlest quavering timeless
woe. It seemed
the real and only sanity to me.

GARY COPELAND LILLEY, Poet

Regarding Chainsaws

Hayden Carruth
Collected Shorter Poems, 1946–1991 (1992)

The first chainsaw I owned was years ago,
an old yellow McCulloch that wouldn't start.
Bo Bremmer give it to me that was my friend,
though I've had enemies couldn't of done
no worse. I took it to Ward's over to Morrisville,
and no doubt they tinkered it as best they could,
but it still wouldn't start. One time later
I took it down to the last bolt and gasket
and put it together again, hoping somehow
I'd do something accidental-like that would
make it go, and then I yanked on it
450 times, as I figured afterwards,
and give myself a bursitis in the elbow
that went five years even after
Doc Arrowsmith shot it full of cortisone
and near killed me when he hit a nerve
dead on. Old Stan wanted that saw, wanted it bad.
Figured I was a greenhorn that didn't know
nothing and he could fix it. Well, I was,
you could say, being only forty at the time,
but a fair hand at tinkering. "Stan," I said,
"you're a neighbor. I like you. I wouldn't
sell that thing to nobody, except maybe
Vice-President Nixon." But Stan persisted.
He always did. One time we was loafing and
gabbing in his front dooryard, and he spied
that saw in the back of my pickup. He run
quick inside, then come out and stuck a double
sawbuck in my shirt pocket, and he grabbed
that saw and lugged it off. Next day, when I
drove past, I seen he had it snugged down tight
with a tow-chain on the bed of his old Dodge
Powerwagon, and he was yanking on it
with both hands. Two or three days after,
I asked him, "How you getting along with that
McCulloch, Stan?" "Well," he says, "I tooken
it down to scrap, and I buried it in three

separate places yonder on the upper side
of the potato piece. You can't be too careful,"
he says, "when you're disposing of a hex."
The next saw I had was a godawful ancient
Homelite that I give Dry Dryden thirty bucks for,
temperamental as a ram too, but I liked it.
It used to remind me of Dry and how he'd
clap that saw a couple times with the flat
of his double-blade axe to make it go
and how he honed the chain with a worn-down
file stuck in an old baseball. I worked
that saw for years. I put up forty-five
run them days each summer and fall to keep
my stoves het through the winter. I couldn't now.
It'd kill me. Of course they got these here
modern Swedish saws now that can take
all the worry out of it. What's the good
of that? Takes all the fun out too, don't it?
Why, I reckon. I mind when Gilles Boivin snagged
an old sap spout buried in a chunk of maple
and it tore up his mouth so bad he couldn't play
"Tea for Two" on his cornet in the town band
no more, and then when Toby Fox was holding
a beech limb that Rob Bowen was bucking up
and the saw skidded crossways and nipped off
one of Toby's fingers. Ain't that more like it?
Makes you know you're living. But mostly they wan't
dangerous, and the only thing they broke was your
back. Old Stan, he was a buller and a jammer
in his time, no two ways about that, but he
never sawed himself. Stan had the sugar
all his life, and he wan't always too careful
about his diet and the injections. He lost
all the feeling in his legs from the knees down.
One time he started up his Powerwagon
out in the barn, and his foot slipped off the clutch,
and she jumped forwards right through the wall
and into the manure pit. He just set there,
swearing like you could of heard it in St.
Johnsbury, till his wife come out and said,
"Stan, what's got into you?" "Missus," he says
"ain't nothing got into me. Can't you see?
It's me that's got into this here pile of shit."
Not much later they took away one of his
legs, and six months after that they took

the other and left him setting in his old chair
with a tank of oxygen to sip at whenever
he felt himself sinking. I remember that chair.
Stan reupholstered it with an old bearskin
that must of come down from his great-great-
grandfather and had grit in it left over
from the Civil War and a bullet-hole as big
as a yawning cat. Stan latched the pieces together
with rawhide, cross fashion, but the stitches was
always breaking and coming undone. About then
I quit stopping by to see old Stan, and I
don't feel so good about that neither. But my mother
was having her strokes then. I figured
one person coming apart was as much
as a man can stand. Then Stan was taken away
to the nursing home, and then he died. I always
remember how he planted them pieces of spooked
McCulloch up above the potatoes. One time
I went up and dug, and I took the old
sprocket, all pitted and et away, and set it
on the windowsill right there next to the
butter mold. But I'm damned if I know why.

A world-renowned marine biologist, Bob Francis worked for many years as a volunteer for Copper Canyon Press. He installed his Poetry Post overlooking Port Townsend Bay. During his wife Kathy's illness, he would often post their shared favorites for the enjoyment of strangers, friends, and tourists who were afforded a glimpse into the poems that filled their house.

On poem 16 by Cold Mountain (Han Shan), translated from the Chinese by Red Pine

I bought *The Collected Songs of Cold Mountain* for my dad for Christmas when I was twenty-one. It had come out that year, and it was the first poetry book I'd ever given anyone. It was also the year I had decided to try to write poems of my own. I knew he would love it (my dad kept, for almost all of my childhood, a copy of Matthiessen's *The Snow Leopard* on his nightstand), but this edition of *Cold Mountain* initiated a now twenty-plus-year conversation about poetry between us, which was the best part of the gift, of course. The poem itself reads almost like Cold Mountain's title track—a poem where he shows off not only his name, trademark humility, and self-awareness but also his unique understanding of nature and the world.

NATHANIEL PERRY, APR/Honickman First Book Prize winner

On "*Shin:* Instruction for Lighting Fires" by Emily Warn

Emily Warn's "Instruction for Lighting Fires" vicariously captures a night of my own life that proved to be transformative. When facing a personal crisis, I ran to the only place in the world I could be certain would offer me solace: a wilderness lake where I tended a small stick fire that I fed with twigs throughout the night. I sat in solitude with pain and loss, watching galaxies swirl by overhead, the sound of waves lapping at the shore. Like all of Emily's poems, this one pares the experience down to its uncluttered essence, where, through her faithful, sublime witness, she disappears, offering the reader a portal into their own intimate experience, the opportunity for transcendence, healing—for me—and, ultimately, the path home.

GEORGE KNOTEK, Copublisher and Development Director

On "Splitting an Order" by Ted Kooser

When my wife, Kathy, and I both entered our seventies, we realized that a full meal at a restaurant was too much. So we started splitting an order and sharing. In fact, what we learned is that there is a substantial amount of ceremony that comes with splitting an order. And that is what Ted Kooser so beautifully captures in "Splitting an Order."

BOB FRANCIS, Volunteer

When I first picked up Bob Hicok's *Red Rover Red Rover*, I opened the book randomly and came upon "Once more, from the top." The poem struck a nerve immediately. I love the lines "Gone are the pulleys, orchestras, / moons."

JEFFREY BISHOP, Board Member

Once more, from the top

Bob Hicok
Red Rover Red Rover (2020)

Sex has changed for my wife and me as we get older.
The less of it contrasts with the better of it.
It's also simpler. Gone are the pulleys, orchestras,
moons. Sometimes we just look at each other in the kitchen
doing dishes or say *Zanzibar* simultaneously and have orgasms
or remember our best ones and shout those dates
at the spoons or whatever else looks like an ear.
I don't recall my first orgasm or my first time
down a slide or the first time I robbed a bank
or the first time today I realized I wasn't breathing
and took a series of deep breaths to catch up.
Let's bury *The Book of Why We're So Nervous*
up to its neck and pour honey over it
so ants will devour our problems and one
or more of us can get gluten-free pizza for the group
to celebrate our symbolic defeat
over our resemblance to insects in terms
of how crushable we are. I mean, if you want to.
My wife and I could also meet you for drinks
and not bring up the sex stuff or the crushing nature
of existence stuff, or even better, for bocce ball
with an old deaf Italian man who'll explain the game
by acting out the Thirty Years' War, as if life
is but a competition for space
when it's also a competition for clever desserts
and intimacy. Like right now, the me
who wants to write this poem about loving my wife
is fighting the me who wants to actually love my wife
by greeting her this morning as she wakes
as slowly as a sack of potatoes growing eyes.
That sounds mean but that's really how she wakes.
Which reminds me that *organic* is one of the few words
that sounds like *orgasmic,* which is one of the few words

54 || Come Shining

I hate to say, like *moist* or *ouch* or *death,*
which reminds me that telling the truth is important
but my question has always been, Tell the truth what,
other than go away and leave us alone.

On "The Snow Country" by Robert Hedin

Robert Hedin's "The Snow Country" is the poem that first brought the name Copper Canyon to my vocabulary, where it has since held a shining spot. As has the poetry of Bert Hedin: careful, humane, generous, honest, sweet, deep.

RICHARD KENNEY, Board Member

On "Sunset on 14th Street" by Alex Dimitrov

This summer, I read "Sunset on 14th Street" to a bunch of middle-aged white dudes, who are decidedly not poetry lovers, around a campfire in an RV park in eastern Oregon. I was channeling Dimitrov's obstinacy and trying to gain the upper hand. I was shocked that they "got it." They were moved by this urgent call to action—to live, like, now. We all eventually returned to our respective motor homes, but for a moment we were cosmic pilgrims riding the same wavelength. These poems are for everyone, even if you don't live in New York.

HAILEY GAUNT, Intern

On "The Wreck of the Great Northern" by Robert Hedin

The first time I read Robert Hedin's "The Wreck of the Great Northern," I was at first certain I had read it before. The haunting images of the Pullman cars full of passengers now stilled in the spectral depth and flow of an impassive river reawakened something I had repressed for years. And I realized I had not read the poem before, I had been in it myself. Years before, as a brakeman for the Chicago and Northwestern Railroad, I had been called out of bed one night to serve on a crew cleaning up the ruin of a freight train that had spilled off the tracks in the western suburbs of Chicago. It was not the tragic wreck of that Great Northern train with all the lives it took, but I can verify that Robert's faithful rendering of that otherworldly, surreal devastation does what all good poems do, putting the reader in the heart of what Jim Harrison called the "human heat" of the experience.

GEORGE KNOTEK, Copublisher and Development Director

This poem always makes me think of the Cabela's parking lot in Olympia. I would drive down from Port Townsend once a month to hand my toddler off to his father for the week. Lucia, like so many of the amazing poets in the Copper Canyon Press family, didn't just name the unnameable. She also gave it depth and beauty, weaving golden threads through the good, bad, and ugly of life.

TONAYA ROSENBERG, Managing Editor

To the Field of Scotch Broom That Will Be Buried by the New Wing of the Mall
Lucia Perillo
On the Spectrum of Possible Deaths (2012)

Half costume jewel, half parasite, you stood
swaying to the music of cash registers in the distance
while a helicopter chewed the linings
of the clouds above the clear-cuts.
And I forgave the pollen count
while cabbage moths teased up my hair
before your flowers fell apart when they
turned into seeds. How resigned you were
to your oblivion, unlistening to the cumuli
as they swept past. And soon those gusts
will mill you, when the backhoe comes
to dredge your roots, but that is not
what most impends, as the chopper descends
to the hospital roof so that somebody's heart
can be massaged back into its old habits.

Mine went a little haywire
at the crest of the road, on whose other side
you lay in blossom.
As if your purpose were to defibrillate me
with a thousand electrodes,
one volt each.

Hearing Richard Siken read "War of the Foxes" just stopped me in my tracks. Poems are to be treasured and poets maybe more so. They bring us words that quicken the pulse of experience just at the edge of understanding. A gift.

VINCENT BUCK, Board Member

War of the Foxes

Richard Siken
War of the Foxes (2015)

I

Two rabbits were chased by a fox, of all the crazy shit in the world, and the fox kept up the chase, circling the world until the world caught up with them in some broken-down downtown metropolis. Inside the warren, the rabbits think fast. Pip touches the only other rabbit listening.

Pip: We're doomed.
Flip: We're not.
Pip: Are you sure?
Flip: Yes. Here, hide inside me.

This is the story of Pip and Flip, the bunny twins. We say that once there were two and now there is only one. When the fox sees Pip run past, he won't know that the one is inside the other. He'll think, *Well, there's at least one more rabbit in that warren.* But no one's left. You know this and I know this. Together we trace out the trail away from doom. There isn't hope, there is a trail. I follow you.

When a rabbit meets a rabbit, one takes the time to tell the other this story. The rabbits then agree there must be two rabbits, at least two rabbits, and that in turn there is a trace. I am only repeating what I heard. This is one love. There are many loves but only one war.

Bird 1: This is the same story.
Bird 2: No, this is the rest of the story.

2

Let me tell you a story about war. A man found his life to be empty. He began to study Latin. Latin was difficult for the man to understand. *I will study Latin, even though it is difficult,* said the man. *Yes, even if it is difficult.*

Let me tell you a story about war. A man had a dream about a woman and then he met her. The man had a dream about the woman's former lover. The former lover was sad, he wanted to fight. The man said to the woman, *I will have to comfort your former lover or I will always be fighting him in my dreams. Yes,* said the woman. *You will need to comfort him, or we will never be finished with this.*

Let me tell you a story about war. A fisherman's son and his dead brother sat on the shore. *That is my country and this is your country and the line in the sand is the threshold between them,* said the dead brother. *Yes,* said the fisherman's son.

You cannot have an opponent if you keep saying yes.

Bird 1: This is the wrong story.
Bird 2: All stories are the wrong story when you are impatient.

Let me tell you a story about war. A man says to another man, *Can I tell you something?* The other man says, *No.* A man says to another man, *There is something I have to tell you. No,* says the other man. *No, you don't.*

Bird 1: Now we are getting somewhere.
Bird 2: Yes, yes we are.

3

Let me tell you a story about war:

A boy spills a glass of milk and his father picks him up by the back of the shirt and throws him against the wall. *You killed my wife and you can't even keep a glass on the table.* The wife had died of sadness, by her own hand. The father walks out of the room and the room is almost empty.

The road outside the house lies flat on the ground. The ground surrenders.

The father works late. The dead wife's hand makes fishsticks while the boy sits in the corner where he fell. The fish in the fishsticks think to themselves, *This is not what we meant to be.*

Its roots in the ground and its branches in the air, a tree is pulled in two directions.

The wife has a dead hand. This is earlier. She is living and her dead hand feeds her pills that don't work. The boy sleeps on the roof or falls out of trees. The father works late. The wife looks out the window and thinks, *Not this.*

The boy is a bird, bad bird. He falls out of trees.

4

Let me tell you a story about war:

The fisherman's son serves drinks to sailors. He stands behind the bar. He listens closely for news of his dead brother. The sailors are thirsty. They drink rum. *Tell me a story,* says the fisherman's son.

There is nothing interesting about the sea. The water is flat, flat and calm, it seems a sheet of glass. You look at it, the more you look at it the more you feel like you are looking into your own head, which is a stranger's head, empty. We listen to the sound with our equipment. I have learned to understand this sound. When you look there is nothing, with the equipment there is sound. We sit in rows and listen down the tunnels for the song. The song has red words in it. We write them down on sheets of paper and pass them along. Sometimes there is noise and sometimes song and often there is silence, the long tunnel, the sea like glass . . .

You are a translator, says the fisherman's son.
Yes, says the sailor.
And the sound is the voice of the enemy.
Yes, yes it is.

5

Let me tell you a story about love:

She had a soft voice and strong hands. When she sang she would seem too large for the room and she would play guitar and sing, which would make his chest feel huge. Sometimes he would touch her knee and smile. Sometimes she would touch his face and close her eyes.

6

The fisherman's son is a spy, a good one. Spies like documents. Spies wander and roam, scanning the information.

A man does work. A machine can, too. Power of agency, agent of what? This is a question we might ask.

What is a document before it's a document? A noise in your head, a backstory. What makes a thing yours to steal or sell or trade? That is a question, good question.

Spies are pollinators. They take the bits from here and there to make a new thing grow. Does it matter to which team this new thing belongs?

7

Fox rounds the warren but there are no bunnies, jumps up with claws but there are no bunnies, moves down the road but there are no bunnies. There are no bunnies. He chases a bird instead. All wars are the same war. The bird flies away.

8

The fisherman's son knows nothing worth stealing. Perhaps, perhaps.

He once put a cat in a cardboard box, but she got out anyway. He once had a brother he lost to the sea. Brother, dead brother, who speaks to him in dreams. These are a few things worth saying.

He knows that when you snap a mast it's time to get a set of oars or learn how to breathe underwater. Rely on one thing too long and when it disappears and you have nothing—well, that's just bad planning. It's embarrassing, to think it could never happen. It happens.

You cannot get in the way of anyone's path to God. You can, but it does no good. Every spy knows this. Some say God is where we put our sorrow. God says, *Which one of you fuckers can get to me first?*

9

The spies meet at the chain-link fence and tell each other stories. A whisper system, a level of honesty. To testify against yourself is an interesting thing, a sacrifice. Some people do it. Some people find money in the street, but you can't rely on it. The fisherman's son is at the fence, waiting to see if he is useful.

You cannot get in the way of anyone's path to happiness, it also does no good. The problem is figuring out which part is the path and which part is the happiness.

It's a blessing: every day someone shows up at the fence. And when no one shows up, a different kind of blessing. In the wrong light anyone can look like a darkness.

People like to say that a good poem makes the familiar strange, but, just as often, a good poem helps us to see what makes the familiar seem familiar. There are few things we hold as close to ourselves as our own hands; Jim Richardson shows us why, and, how, and how much.

DAVID ORR, Poet

On the One Hand and on the Other

James Richardson
For Now (2020)

Consider the palms. They are faces
with their eyes closed, the ten spread fingers
soft exclamations, sadness or surprise.
They have smile lines and sorrow lines, like faces.
Like faces, they can be hard to read.

Somehow my palms, though they have held my life
piece by piece, seem young and pale.
So much has touched them, nothing has remained.
They are innocent, maybe, though they guess
they have a darker side that they cannot grasp.

The backs of my hands, indeed, are so different,
shadowy from the sun, all bones and strain,
that sometimes I think they are not mine.
But time on my hands, blood on my hands—
for such things I have never blamed my hands.

One hand writes. Sometimes it writes a reminder
on the other hand, which knows it will never write,
though it has learned, in secret, how to type.
That is sad, perhaps, but the dominant hand is sadder,
with its fear that it will never, not really, be written on.

They are like an old couple at home. All day,
each knows exactly where the other is.
They must speak, though how is a mystery,
so rarely do they touch, so briefly come together,
now and then to wash, maybe in prayer.

I consider my hands, palms up. *Empty,* I say,
though it is exactly then that they are weighing
not a particular stone or loaf I have chosen
but everything, everything, the whole tall world,
finding it light, finding it light as air.

On "Sunflower" by Rolf Jacobsen, translated from the Norwegian by Robert Bly

Rolf Jacobsen's "Sunflower" inspires me to yearn for what's down the road instead of fear it and to foster my own growth always. Its Norwegian origins are also of special ancestral value to me. The world needs more Norwegian translations!

CLAYTON HASELWOOD, Intern

On "Grief" by Matthew Dickman

Matthew Dickman's "Grief" gets grief right, the grotesque distortions and unnerving insistence of loss. Many poems are about how sad grief is—everyone already knows that. What Dickman shows in this poem is how ridiculous and impossible to shake it is, how it's a kind of love affair, a kind of animal.

ED SKOOG, Poet

On "Distracted by an Ergonomic Bicycle" by James Arthur

I heard James read this poem, somewhere in Seattle, during my time as an intern. At that point in my life, having just graduated college and living in this strange place with long-lasting winter nights, I felt buffeted and carried in ways I couldn't control—unmoored. The consolation offered in "Distracted by an Ergonomic Bicycle," its intervention, simply states that distraction might be enough, that close attention to the surrounding world might keep us going.

NOAH LLOYD, Intern

On "America" by Victoria Chang

My favorite poem in *Obit* is "America." Death is, as Wallace Stevens said, "the mother of beauty," and in this poem, death is Kafkaesque: the place where "children hold telegrams they must hand to a woman at a desk." And yet, Chang's mother is there, "taking in all the children." The delicacy of the exchange Chang imagines between the world of the dead and our world is beautiful. The fact that it is "America" that is dead here is prophetic. I love the way this poem dances with the idea of "witness" poetry yet remains, essentially, a lyric poem about poetry's most urgent topics, love—in this case maternal love—and death.

GAIL WRONSKY, Poet

On "Berryman" by W.S. Merwin

W.S. Merwin's "Berryman" is pinned over my desk to remind me that the fluttering in my chest when the day's work is done is not the singing of the muse, it's probably a heart attack.

ART HANLON, Associate Editor, Volunteer, and Intern

On "The River of Bees" by W.S. Merwin

I became obsessed with Merwin's "The River of Bees" having read it in an anthology while I was living, and often languishing in depression, in Russia. I was particularly enchanted by the magical disjunction of the poem, where images flow into statements and back again; it's as if the poet is an oracle, receiving messages from the spirit world, where death meets life. The final lines gave me courage to realize that though I was going through a period of real suffering, as long as I could live through and not merely survive it, I would bear the fruit of that struggle. It was a year I never forgot, and it helped shape the poet and person I am today. Merwin was there with me. Soon it will be thirty years. "But we were not born to survive / Only to live."

PHILIP METRES, Poet

I still remember when "Solitaire" knocked me out. I read it for the first time in the *New Yorker* before it was adapted for *The Uses of the Body*. I was jealous.

ALEX DIMITROV, Poet

from "Minutes, Years"
Deborah Landau
The Uses of the Body (2015)

~

One summer there was no girl left in me.
It gradually became clear.
It suddenly became.

In the pool, I was more heavy than light.
Pockmarked and flabby in a floppy hat.

What will my body be
when parked all night in the earth?

Midsummer.
Breathe in. Breathe out.

I am not on the oxygen tank.
Twice a week we have sex.

The lithe girls poolside I see them
at their weddings I see them with babies their hips
thickening I see them middle-aged.

I can't see past the point where I am.
Like you, I'm just passing through.

After a summer where I couldn't celebrate Pride due to the pandemic, I came to this poem during the fall of 2020. In its remembrance of queer ecstasy all the way back in 1992, it provided a tender balm I didn't know I needed.

REUBEN GELLEY NEWMAN, Intern

Gay Pride Weekend, S.F., 1992
Brenda Shaughnessy
So Much Synth (2016)

I forgot how lush and electrified
it was with you. The shaggy
fragrant zaps continually passing
back and forth, my fingertip
to your clavicle, or your wrist
rubbing mine to share gardenia
oil. We so purred like dragonflies
we kept the mosquitoes away
and the conversation was heavy,
mother-lacerated childhoods
and the sad way we'd both
been both ignored and touched
badly. Knowing that being
fierce and proud and out and
loud was just a bright new way
to be needy. *Please listen to me,* oh
what a buzz! *you're the only one
I can tell.* Even with no secret,
I could come close to your ear
with my mouth and that was
ecstasy, too. We barely touched
each other, we didn't have to
speak. The love we made leapt
to life like a cat in the space
between us (if there ever *was*
space between us), and looked
back at us through fog. Sure,
this was San Francisco, it was
often hard to see. But fog always
burned off, too, so we watched
this creature to see if it knew
what it was doing. It didn't.

I came to Akwaeke Emezi's *Content Warning: Everything* right as I began seriously working on my MFA thesis, a graphic memoir navigating my struggles with sexual trauma. I remember, in an interview with Shondaland in 2022, Emezi admitted their sadness as they honestly discussed how content warnings are deeply symbolic of their trauma but connote the possibility of opting out of these experiences, a choice Emezi never had in their life. I resonated with their words so deeply, I was stunned. Never before had I encountered someone who mirrored my own history back to me so completely.

And I was gratified even more so once I had read *Content Warning: Everything* in its entirety. This poem spoke to me particularly. Emezi captures so clearly that rage inherent to the burden, the legacy of sexual trauma— so elemental with the yearning to make the earth quake with retribution. Through Emezi's imaginings of a sad, protective god, vengeful with the desire to make them feel safe, I come close.

JAY AJA, Intern

what if jesus sought vengeance
Akwaeke Emezi
Content Warning: Everything (2022)

my elderdead brother listens to my halfmeal memories
    narrow atrocities in my shower / a magician's hand on the back of my
head / forcing my neck over his reclining cock / he doesn't remember,
he says / he was asleep / a boy in a mountain / plunges in and out /
as the ceiling eats my gaze

the son of god narrows his eyes
    an orchard of figs bursts into fire / dead wasps cloud the air /
fear tastes like a child's forgiveness in my mouth / i have sinned too,
i tell him / there is damp grief in his hands / not like this, he says /
picking up the whip from the sand / not like this

he will not let me in their houses
    tells me this belongs to him / i know nothing of certain wars /
licks the air with his cowhide tongue / the men weep with nowhere to
run / their women press their thighs together / fighting the slick of a
winedark swell

On "disclosure" by Akwaeke Emezi

I first came to know Akwaeke Emezi's voice in *Freshwater*, their debut novel, which begins, "The first time our mother came for us, we screamed." I opened that book and immediately fell head over heels for the radical intelligence of this writer, for their use of plural pronouns to speak a plurality of selves, for prose that is operatic, ecstatic, yet grounded in subtleties, in bodily particulars.

Years later, I sent a note to Akwaeke, thanking them for the work and humbly asking to read a poetry manuscript—if by chance they had written one. Lucky for us, like many visionary cross-genre writers (Ursula K. Le Guin comes to mind) Akwaeke had been writing poetry long before they became known for fiction and memoir.

The poem "disclosure" sends me back to that first sentence from *Freshwater*. The personal milestone of "coming out" is culturally regarded as a birth of sorts (or death, for some), though any queer person knows it's not a singular moment or linear path. This poem runs breathlessly sans punctuation from origin to insult, revelation to freedom, inviting readers to hold complexity through overlapping syntax, intersecting identities, and the gorgeous co-arising of hurt and loved selves—"who knew i could love me so loudly."

ELAINA ELLIS, Editor

Recommended by **ELAINA ELLIS**,
Editor

Objects in Mirror Are Closer Than They Appear

Michael Wasson
Swallowed Light (2022)

Awake again, I find my name as
                     vanished as a midnight I want
     to salvage. To have those black teeth sinking back
                           into my skin—you enter me
through an opening in the sky
             of my body like a face,

      a moon behind me falling slow
                 & moving its fingers to a mirror made
of the window above my bed. I hear the weight of its life
                   pressing down & the image
     cracks. A figure stands
         in a gown of blued smoke—this *me*
                & *you*—a shadow laid over
        the surface of a puddle. Its eyes

              lit up like those
of wolves brimming with winter. So let this body. Let it go:
               as though a breath
     wanted to be saved, I part my mouth into
            púuceyxceyxne & *into pieces*
as I am. But language between the lips
           shrapneled into air is all that ever touches
     the never-seen

     pink of my lungs. I breathe in & breathe out. For what
            we've lost—my dear
ghosts. The sound of the field
        long after the war

I obtained James Masao Mitsui's *Journal of the Sun* while at Copper Canyon Press in one of the many generous offers to peruse the catalogue. I couldn't read this collection until the end of 2021, and, when I did, I found Mitsui's careful, striking meditations and bold truths to give a direction out of what had been another anxious year since the novel coronavirus first broke out. Wanting and striving have become tenacious conditions when the face of death looms over and around us. I found myself re-centered by "Sunday Drive, the Autumn Leaf Festival"—the poem travels through the seasons in an attempt to reorient one to the present. The last four lines are guiding me into the new year.

ZUHRA AMINI, Intern

Sunday Drive, the Autumn Leaf Festival

James Masao Mitsui
Journal of the Sun (1974)

for Jan Coleman

Tomorrow will be the kind of day for windows.
To look at a distant place
where you've been, the trees making the sun come out
when it's cloudy. Fall is a beginning;
it's sensing the frozen air, an earlier sunset.
Crisp leaves turn, the smell burning into winter.

Winter is a long distance; it is everything
we don't know. Everyone has a different way to travel.
We won't find it until our lives are put together
and we've stopped looking back.
From here the ridges are white-capped waves;
hot days belong to another year.

When we come to spring it won't be where we think.
It will gently open in the trees.
We will want to stop, not go on,
just stay at the side of the road like a crow
and watch others trying to travel.

I've decided to let the way just happen.
Forcing it would bring another winter.
I want the sun, a horse grazing his choice of grass
without having to fear fences. There is no line
dividing seasons; they happen as we let them.

On "Death of a Child" by Jenny George

Like much of Jenny George's work, "Death of a Child" is suffused with a stillness, a stillness that lies in the center of upheaval and transformation. The title is spare and chilling, yet the poem is full of renewal and pulses with life. Things are constantly becoming other things. Ordinary occurrences like birth and death—whether of a child or a star—become miraculous under the author's careful attention, and we are led to wonder, "Can you hold it still forever?" This poem reminds us that life is a current of change that carries us endlessly forward: "Aimed / at death, we live. We keep on / doing this."

JANEEN ARMSTRONG, Intern Program Manager and Reader Services Manager

Jenny George's debut collection, *The Dream of Reason,* came out the week my son would have turned twenty. I was three and a half years into mourning his loss and during this time, poetry had become an essential tool to my survival. In both reading and writing poetry, I was beginning to find language for an experience that seemed entirely outside of language.

Jenny's collection spoke deeply to me at this critical time in my life. In her imagination, the natural world and particularly the animal world was one of joy and violence and beauty. Her images and metaphors aligned with my own interior landscape of rage, hope, loss, and love. I read *The Dream of Reason* over and over, and each time I felt just a little less alone in my grief. But in each reading, I skipped over her poem "Death of a Child." I was too raw, and the poem felt too hot.

When asked to contribute a poem to this anthology, I knew I wanted to choose from *The Dream of Reason.* I sat down once again to encounter the collection, but this time I was ready to read "Death of a Child." In it, Jenny translated the angles of my grief. She writes of the current through the cornfield, the collapse of the stars and the light that comes through the dark passages. She says, "I can't explain it. I can't explain it," then somehow, miraculously, does.

LAURIE EUSTIS, Board Member

I read Galvin for the first time while working at New Dominion Bookshop in Charlottesville, an hour before closing time. My friend and coworker, the poet Hodges Adams, handed me *X*, and while I can't remember what poem the book was opened to, any one of them would have done the trick. The book floored me, literally; I spent the remainder of my shift sitting on the floor, devouring it whole. Like Galvin, "my categorical / imperative is falling in love." By the end of the book, I had readily done so. My infinite gratitude to Copper Canyon for publishing poetry that's so easy to fall into and in love with.

JAY BAKER, Intern

Nature Averts Her Eyes

James Galvin
X (2003)

> Fool. *He's mad that trusts in the*
> *tameness of a wolf, a horse's*
> *health, a boy's love, or a whore's*
> *oath.*
>
> King Lear

Fool. I had an exaggerated interest in death, so much so it was possible I might already be dead.
Anyway, I had this ridiculous feeling that I could walk around, that I had found my wallet, that a beautiful woman had kissed me twice, once on each of the lenses of my spectacles.
No, that's wrong.
Actually I was someone else.

Could it be you?
Is causality a structure?
Nothing happens that is supposed to happen, of that I am certain.
Probability cannot be enthusiastic, only the unlikely can.
Your voice is velvety.
Watch out.
I have inspected my restored order and find it wanting, insipid even.
I'm getting drowsy, a good sign.

Yesterday was different.
I
tried to convince myself that passion was not a gyre of dust
swirling about my feet.
Would you like a biscuit?
I lived in a
lukewarm province until it became unbearable.
I touched
everything.
It didn't help.
The room insists.
My categorical
imperative is falling in love.
I saw a ship dancing on waves.
It even
kicked up its heels.
It heeled over.
That ship will never sink alone,
without a captain.
Scientific aspirations, curiously inaccurate,
unrolled before the innocents.
The subject had arisen.
Something
like happiness had long since lost my other.
Dark eyes staring into
ice-blue ones.
I do not want to know how old the stars are.
I do not
want to know how long they have left on their astral death row.
As
if they really existed, like gods.
What's their point?
It was very
quiet in the Faculty Club as, outside, the firing squad took aim.

Lightning's alphabet.
Little circles, sightless, float down the river to
the sky.

Recommended by **MARY JANE KNECHT**, Development Director and Managing Editor

Winter Road

James Galvin
Lethal Frequencies (1995)

The reasons the winter road acts so crazy
Are all invisible now.

The summer road persists
In reasoned argument,
Reducing terrain to topography,

Curving gracefully to the left,
Or bending gently to the right,

Gaining, falling, abstracting
Rises, draws, outcrops, woods.

The winter road is crazy.
This time of year it seems
To slam nihilistically

Against the ridgeside,
Sidle through unlikely groves,

Make esses where the summer road goes straight,
Crossing and recrossing,

It dodges to the left, leaps to the right,
A road out of control.

In winter how a road should go
Is told by contours of atmosphere.

The landscape is just a situation
Of windbreaks and wind-permissions.

Heedlessly the summer road
Dives into broad drifts.

It surfaces a couple of times
Between white waves,
Then goes down for good.

Now the winter road is smart to seek
High ground, exposed to the wind,

To thread the drifts
Like big white corpses on a field.

Come winter this road proves amazing.
All along it was
In the right place,

Already leaping to the left,
Dodging to the right,

Sailing through contours of atmosphere,
Prophetic and dumb.

Jaan Kaplinski was a major European poet who deserved and deserves more readers over here in the United States. When I first read him, the minimalism rang clear and true for me.

MICHAEL WHITE, Poet

We started home, my son and I

Jaan Kaplinski, translated from the Estonian
by the author with Sam Hamill and Riina Tamm
The Wandering Border (1987)

We started home, my son and I.
Twilight already. The young moon
stood in the western sky and beside it
a single star. I showed them to my son
and explained how the moon should be greeted
and that this star is the moon's servant.
As we neared home, he said
that the moon is far, as far
as that place where we went.
I told him the moon is much, much farther
and reckoned: if one were to walk
ten kilometers each day, it would take
almost a hundred years to reach the moon.
But this was not what he wanted to hear.
The road was already almost dry.
The river was spread on the marsh; ducks and other waterfowl
crowed the beginning of night. The snow's crust
crackled underfoot—it must
have been freezing again. All the houses' windows
were dark. Only in our kitchen
a light shone. Beside our chimney, the shining moon,
and beside the moon, a single star.

On "There Is a Light in Me" by Anna Swir, translated from the Polish by Czesław Miłosz and Leonard Nathan

My father traveled three thousand miles to Port Townsend, Washington, to visit his young granddaughters. One evening, after the girls were in bed, we sat around the kitchen table talking, laughing, and telling stories. At one point Grandpa asked, with genuine curiosity, "How do you read a poem?" Pause. Breath. This question from a man who never sought out poems, but who was trying to understand what his publisher son did for a living. "Oh, Dad, simple. Just read a poem like you would a letter to the editor." Then I found *Talking to My Body* by Anna Swir, a brilliant Polish poet, who served as a nurse during the Warsaw Uprising in World War II. I knew my dad had a fascination with both Eastern Europe and World War II. I opened the book randomly and read a poem aloud, something about a railway station and a woman seeking shelter. "Can I borrow that book?" he asked. "And can I borrow a pad of sticky notes? I want to mark the poems I want to come back to." Turns out, Grandpa stayed up reading until two in the morning, finished the book in one sitting, sticky notes on nearly every page. His heart cracked wide open.

JOSEPH BEDNARIK, Copublisher and Marketing Director

On "Poem After Carlos Drummond de Andrade" by Marvin Bell

Marvin Bell was a hero of mine when I was in high school and was also one of the first poets I met when working as an intern at Copper Canyon Press. I love this poem because it dares to offer wisdom, it is beautiful while utilizing common language, and it nods to the international reach at the core of Copper Canyon Press's catalogue and mission.

JEREMY VOIGT, Website Proofreader and Intern

On "Telemachus" by Ocean Vuong

I read Ocean Vuong's poem "Telemachus" for the first time several years ago, on a beach in Puerto Vallarta the morning after my husband, Dean, had been admitted to the hospital with a life-threatening lower GI bleed. The poem filled me with grief and longing and brought me to tears. Dean survived this medical scare, but this poem still reminds me how the difficulties of life—losing loved ones, strained family relationships—through poetry can become mythic, can be transformed into art.

PETER PEREIRA, Poet

Vuong's work has routinely provided me such permission to grow, to morph. Vuong asks, "Dearest father, what becomes of the boy / no longer a boy?" And finally I was able to ask myself, what becomes of the girl, no longer a girl? A true gift.

KAYLEB RAE CANDRILLI, Poet

Prayer for the Newly Damned

Ocean Vuong
Night Sky with Exit Wounds (2016)

Dearest Father, forgive me for I have seen.
Behind the wooden fence, a field lit
with summer, a man pressing a shank
to another man's throat. Steel turning to light
on sweat-slick neck. Forgive me
for not twisting this tongue into the shape
of Your name. For thinking:
this must be how every prayer
begins—the word *Please* cleaving
the wind into fragments, into what
a boy hears in his need to know
how pain blesses the body back
to its sinner. The hour suddenly
stilled. The man, his lips pressed
to the black boot. Am I wrong to love
those eyes, to see something so clear
& blue—beg to remain clear
& blue? Did my cheek twitch
when the wet shadow bloomed from his crotch
& trickled into ochre dirt? How quickly
the blade becomes You. But let me begin
again: There's a boy kneeling
in a house with every door kicked open
to summer. There's a question corroding
his tongue. A knife touching
Your finger lodged inside the throat.
Dearest Father, what becomes of the boy
no longer a boy? *Please*—
what becomes of the shepherd
when the sheep are cannibals?

Re: The Essential Ruth Stone:

whats the word for "in
your 50s, you meet a
voice you've never heard but
it knows you! And it makes
you psyched to go on
to 60, 70, etc."?

KuoXoxox

How Poems Move

On "Curtains" by Ruth Stone

I suppose it was the utter emotional bravery that first struck me about Ruth Stone's "Curtains." The last blunt line feels like a slap across the face that makes you go zero at the bone. The way the single-word title supports the literal quotidian elements of the poem's narrative but also contains a kind of black, almost slapstick, humor (as in "It's curtains for you!"). In twenty-five lines, Stone paints the picture of a marriage, her own frailties, and the anger that so often accompanies grief.

TINA SCHUMANN, Grant Writer and Intern

On "Argument of Situations" by Shangyang Fang

"Argument of Situations" is the first poem in Shangyang Fang's debut, *Burying the Mountain*. And what a stunner! It taught me again how big a poem can be. It's a tour de force poem that begins with lovemaking and unrolls like a scroll into philosophy, aesthetics, spirituality, and geography. Endlessly transformative and packed with beautiful imagery, strange paradoxes, and sexy intimacies, this poem is more than rapturous and gentle: it's as magical as a person.

JANE MILLER, Poet

On "From Up Here" by James Richardson

James Richardson consistently explodes the ordinary with perfect words, and "From Up Here" is no exception. Of course the doors of a bus gasp open and sigh shut! We've all heard those sounds a million times but never knew their names. The sly leap from the dispersing passengers into the wind "that blows from every way at once" transforms the stopping and starting of a bus into something universal. Such sleight of hand can only be accomplished with absolute lucidity and precision. His aphorisms are miniature masterpieces.

CHASE TWICHELL, Poet and Translator

I love the several shifts of axis here! In a virtuosity of dispositions, the poet's turns of phrase adjust and readjust the reader's perspective.

Whatever we thought was about to follow those opening words—"The water is one thing"—was likeliest to be a distinction of nature. What we probably don't expect is what actually follows: "The water is one thing, and one thing . . ."

Reiteration is not usually multiplication, except in words, which make the present doubly so, in representing. The art of numbers glimmers forth at the outset, composition out of counterpoise, leaping beyond commonplaces. Such is the poet's true occasion: find the commonplaces, and then leap from them. Space and time make the terms less terminal!

Jericho Brown is down for that. And up to it too!

HEATHER MCHUGH, Poet

Crossing

Jericho Brown
The Tradition (2019)

The water is one thing, and one thing for miles.
The water is one thing, making this bridge
Built over the water another. Walk it
Early, walk it back when the day goes dim, everyone
Rising just to find a way toward rest again.
We work, start on one side of the day
Like a planet's only sun, our eyes straight
Until the flame sinks. The flame sinks. Thank God
I'm different. I've figured and counted. I'm not crossing
To cross back. I'm set
On something vast. It reaches
Long as the sea. I'm more than a conqueror, bigger
Than bravery. I don't march. I'm the one who leaps.

I read "climbing" and feel the struggles of womanhood and self-doubt pressed against me. Just as Lucille Clifton does in this poem, I push back "hand over hungry hand." Perhaps the woman preceding the speaker up the "long rope" is the self, or perhaps she is an ancestor showing me where to place a hand. Regardless, I feel inside me both the fear of falling and the desire to climb. I feel the meanings of words shifting too. I admire how "maybe" becomes a resounding "no." I should not have wanted less. This poem lyrically, beautifully, tensely, strikes a match. I, too, feel the "bowl in me / burning to be filled."

ASHLEY E. WYNTER, Editor

climbing

Lucille Clifton
The Book of Light (1993)

a woman precedes me up the long rope,
her dangling braids the color of rain.
maybe I should have had braids.
maybe I should have kept the body i started,
slim and possible as a boy's bone.
maybe i should have wanted less.
maybe i should have ignored the bowl in me
burning to be filled.
maybe i should have wanted less.
the woman passes the notch in the rope
marked Sixty.   i rise toward it, struggling,
hand over hungry hand.

There are a few poems I know will transfix just about any audience. I think it's because of the way their narratives build and break. They're irresistible yet profound. Rhythmic, accessible, and complex. This is one of those poems.

SIERRA GOLDEN, Intern

Because

Ellen Bass
Indigo (2020)

Because the night I gave birth my husband went blind.
Hysterical, I guess you'd call it.

Because there'd been too many people
and then there was no one. Only

this small creature—her tiny cry
no bigger than a sequin.

Because I'd been pushing too many hours.
Even with her soft skull plates shifting,

the collar of my bones too slender.
When I reached down

I could feel the wet wisps of hair of this being living
inside me, but her heart was weakening.

The midwife told me not to push
on the way to the hospital, but I pushed anyway.

This was California in the seventies and I'd have pushed until I died.
The doctor asked for permission to cut

my perineum. So polite, as though he were requesting
the pleasure of the next dance. Then he slid in forceps

skillfully, not a scratch on her temples.
But we left that haven the same night because my husband

didn't believe in hospitals, the baby naked,
wrapped only in a blanket because we both believed

in skin to skin. Because the baby cried
but wouldn't suck.

Because when I started to stand
I started to faint so I had to crawl

to the sterile diapers and pale yellow sleeper
folded inside the brown paper bag I'd baked in the oven.

Because I'm still there on my hands and knees,
deflated belly and ripe breasts, huge dark nipples,

tearing open the stapled bag,
fumbling the ducky pins,

two fingers slipped between the baby's belly
and the thick layers of cotton, the sharp point.

The baby, a stranger,
yet so strangely familiar,

flecks of blood still stuck to her scalp.
Because my husband slept

beside me and I let him sleep.
Because it would be years before I left him.

Now love and grief would be greater
than I ever imagined,

rooted together like north and south,
over and under.

Because I too had been pushed out
into another world

I lay there with the baby whimpering in my arms,
both of us wide awake in the darkness.

Rachel McKibbens writes with incredible intensity, and this poem encapsulates her style and the high stakes that make her writing impossible to look away from. It demands your attention.

KELLY MCLENNON, Intern

one more time, with feeling

Rachel McKibbens
blud (2017)

When I was nineteen
I stole a gun. The drug dealer
next door, blitzed out
of her skull, didn't
see me
pull it from her
kitchen cupboard.

As the California sun
sank below the
foothills, I haunted
the neighborhood,
screaming your
doomed name.
I was ready.
A death-wish Romeo
beneath your bedroom
window. Split once
a neighbor threatened
to call the cops.

I never told you this story.

Not because I regret
what I did, was prepared
to do—those forty-five
minutes of havoc, hunting
down your head.

Back then, I wasn't shit.
Just electrified violence.
All fists, piss & safety pins,
an unwed teenage mother
with no address.

You had parents. Freckles.
A three-story house. I'd listen
to you spit your angsty
fiction while I slept in parks
& ate from garbage cans.

When I learned you were
coveting the man I loved,
I felt my insides darken,
cursed your well-fed
royalty disguised as grit.

Got tired of the forgery,
wanted all the black-eyed
wealth to myself:
BANG, you're dead.

Wish I could say I've put
those days behind me,
that I never fall into
the steel-weight daydream
of a gun's hard lesson.

1995—half my life ago—still,
every time you call
to bitch about your latest
ex-soulmate or DUI,
one more kid taken
from you by the state

I want to tell you
about the only night
you survived.
When something
said *fall asleep*
& you did.

Crashed hard
with a starving bitch
& pistol at the ready,
birds still singing
in the half daylight.

I'll say it here, right now,
one more time, with feeling:
it was the only moment
in this wretched life
a god was on my side.

✐ Swir's poems use minimal language, but their effect is always vast, astounding, and true.

ERIC PANKEY, Poet

Calm Down

Anna Swir, translated from the Polish
by Czesław Miłosz and Leonard Nathan
Talking to My Body (1996)

At night
the telephone rings.
I wake up, terrified.
—Something bad
happened to father.

Calm down—says my daughter.
Grandfather is just fine.
After all, he died
a month ago.

On "Confetti" by Arthur Sze

The opening to "Confetti" is a flash event, a shattering of a thing and the assembly of its fragments into a temporal charm. There's no storyline, just events connected through the poet's pyro-poetic technique. Each event begins with a strike that sparks, blooms, and fades back into our crumbling world—a soldering gun, a glittering constellation.

EMILY WARN, Poet

On "Floating Trees" by C.D. Wright

The ending of C.D. Wright's "Floating Trees"—like all her poem endings—is a surprise and a wonder. She makes you forget where you knew she was heading. The poem has all her daring, originality, giant vocabulary, and razor-sharp sensitivity. It's lighthearted and profound, an expert class in how to write descriptions.

All the while, indirectly and casually, the poem lets us see not merely inside a house, inside a bedroom, but inside someone's soul.

JANE MILLER, Poet

On "To make a life inside, you" by Marianne Boruch

I'm drawn to the interiority of Boruch's poems, "To make a life inside, you" in particular for its sense of line and stanza, each swerve, each image—clear, precise—driving to the white-hot center. Upon each return it asks more of me as a reader, which is what I love most in a good poem.

KERRY JAMES EVANS, Poet

On *13th Balloon* by Mark Bibbins

I've designed books for Copper Canyon for more than twenty years. I admire all the poetry I read from the Press, but, every so often, something comes along that hits hard and deep. Mark Bibbins's *13th Balloon* was that kind of poem. From the moment I read a draft manuscript to the very end of the production process, I was riveted, and deeply moved. His ability to use precise language and wit to create something so achingly beautiful is truly remarkable.

PHIL KOVACEVICH, Book and Pressmark Designer

I love how *13th Balloon* invents and then takes that invention to create more poem. The unfolding of wonder through the imagery of thousands of birds allows the poem to speak about a loss, and then the loss begins to unfold, hatch even.

TYREE DAYE, Poet and APR/
Honickman First Book Prize winner

from *13th Balloon*
Mark Bibbins
13th Balloon (2020)

Imagine a bird who lays her egg

then picks it up and flies without

landing until it hatches

Imagine a thousand

of these birds chopping away

at the soggy light

Since you died a thousand birds

have daily flown through me

each leaving behind an egg

       some of which rotted

some of which hatched

releasing more birds that pecked

at my skull

       but not generating the noise

       and pain one might expect

          It's more like hearing

       someone typing

       an endless suicide note

       in a room at the end

       of a carpeted hall

Always one egg remains in me intact

and each time I yank it out

each time I crack it and crush it and throw
away the shell
      it reappears whole

I pull it out and pull it out

I break it a thousand times
but nothing is ever inside

I carry it and carry it   I do not land

/ / /

"Field Notes on Leaving" is a poem I can read endlessly and always with admiration. Sprawling across several pages, with scatterings of stars, the poem takes on a sort of physical existence. It reads like a diary written in landmarks or a meditation written with stars. It is a vast, well-traveled, and lived-in poem that joins form and content so deliberately. Each page turn feels like searching: for answers, for home, for safety, a "looking everywhere." The poem expertly sets the tone for what is a simultaneously heavy and beautiful collection journeying through ancestors and family, history, leaving and returning. It speaks to me on a deep level.

ASHLEY E. WYNTER, Editor

Field Notes on Leaving

Tyree Daye
Cardinal (2020)

> *geography could not save me*
>
> Jacqueline Joan Johnson quoted by
> Isabel Wilkerson in *The Warmth of
> Other Suns*

*

the North Star is irrelevant

miles and miles above my head

I don't want constellations any nearer

I know there are whole cities all over this country

so bright you can't see the stars

the sky no wider than the heart is wide

*

the night President Obama was elected we danced
in the street of our small university
to My President Is Black   first time on my own
I was bright and felt like I had a father
            every one of us was flying
a blunt passed around   we got lifted

my heart to lift

*

            all the world to explore

if there were stars
            we could hold them

*

        I've never been through airport security
        without being pulled to the side and searched
        to know you can die anywhere
        doesn't feel like flying anywhere

*

I can't go to Canada
and leave my mama here alone

*

if you see me dancing a two-step
I'm sending a starless code
we're escaping everywhere

*

I can't afford to think like Whitman
that whomever I shall meet on the road I shall love
and whoever beholds me shall love me

*

Doing the Dougie   trying to find the ocean
                    looking everywhere

I often think of this poem as a chorus of addition because of the conversation between the mother and brother. And because of the omnipresent-ness of the speaker, who sometimes feels like the devil at the corner of the house.

TYREE DAYE, Poet and APR/
Honickman First Book Prize winner

My Brother at 3 A.M.

Natalie Diaz
When My Brother Was an Aztec (2012)

He sat cross-legged, weeping on the steps
when Mom unlocked and opened the front door.
> *O God,* he said. *O God.*
>> *He wants to kill me, Mom.*

When Mom unlocked and opened the front door
at 3 a.m., she was in her nightgown, Dad was asleep.
> *He wants to kill me,* he told her,
>> looking over his shoulder.

3 a.m. and in her nightgown, Dad asleep,
What's going on? she asked. *Who wants to kill you?*
> He looked over his shoulder.
>> *The devil does. Look at him, over there.*

She asked, *What are you on? Who wants to kill you?*
The sky wasn't black or blue but the green of a dying night.
> *The devil, look at him, over there.*
>> He pointed to the corner house.

The sky wasn't black or blue but the dying green of night.
Stars had closed their eyes or sheathed their knives.
> My brother pointed to the corner house.
>> His lips flickered with sores.

Stars had closed their eyes or sheathed their knives.
O God, I can see the tail, he said. *O God, look.*
> Mom winced at the sores on his lips.
>> *It's sticking out from behind the house.*

O God, see the tail, he said. *Look at the goddamned tail.*
He sat cross-legged, weeping on the front steps.
> Mom finally saw it, a hellish vision, my brother.
>> *O God, O God,* she said.

On "The Present" by W.S. Merwin

I've always loved the ambiguous meaning of the title. Of course, "The Present" refers to a gift, but it also directs us to what that gift is: time itself, present moment after present moment, a phenomenon our two mythic progenitors, Adam and Eve, have never known. It's a gift not without its unbearable difficulties, but our couple doesn't know that yet. What they do know is that they are being expelled from Paradise. They laugh when their hands meet, an elation that will be followed by much sorrow. And yet, it's the elation and the sorrow that will be the stuff of their new lives. They might be exiled into a daunting new dimension of existence, but at least they will still have each other.

THOMAS CENTOLELLA, Poet

On "Voluntary Mutilation" by Jean Follain, translated from the French by W.S. Merwin

I admire Merwin's openness to other language traditions and his willingness to labor as a translator. Follain's poetry excels in its selection of concrete details, its depth, and its brevity.

ALFRED CORN, Poet

On "The Sky" by Natalie Shapero

Natalie Shapero has always struck me as a wily poet, difficult to pin down for the stunning complexity of her poems, despite crafting in what many might call "simple" language. Her poem "The Sky" opens with a provocative existentialism and ends in the grounded mundanity of a drunk man at dinner. I'm in awe, every time, of the way we move from one realm to the next, of the plain embrace of the morbid and absurd, of how Shapero reminds us what's real and what we can hold.

JUSTIN NASH, Intern

Natalie Shapero walks a razor-thin tightrope of humor and sadness in each
of her poems. She pulls it off like no one else can.

KELLY MCLENNON, Intern

"Not Horses" miniaturizes the tensions between humor and darkness,
eternity and the decision to have a child, with a tenderness that spills over
into pathos. That last line will never leave me.

NOAH WARREN, Poet

Not Horses

Natalie Shapero
Hard Child (2017)

What I adore is not horses, with their modern
domestic life span of 25 years. What I adore
is a bug that lives only one day, especially if
it's a terrible day, a day of train derailment or
chemical lake or cop admits to cover-up, a day
when no one thinks of anything else, least of all
that bug. I know how it feels, born as I've been
into these rotting times, as into sin. Everybody's
busy, so distraught they forget to kill me,
and even that won't keep me alive. I share
my home not with horses, but with a little dog
who sees poorly at dusk and menaces stumps,
makes her muscle known to every statue.
I wish she could have a single day of language,
so that I might reassure her *don't be afraid—*
our whole world is dead and so can do you no harm.

This poem is a deeply spiritual interrogation that follows the canonical hours, whose brilliance lies in its fidelity to each hour's traditional theme and its ability to apply those themes to the life of a vulnerable contemporary speaker. Its form—a crown of sonnets—underscores the circularity of human experience, as "the hoped-for / and the happening" cycle through our lives.

LINDA BIERDS, Poet

Quarantine
Malachi Black
Storm Toward Morning (2014)

Lauds

Somehow I am sturdier, more shore
than sea-spray as I thicken through
the bedroom door. I gleam of sickness.
You give me morning, Lord, as you
give earthquake to all architecture.
I can forget.
             You put that sugar
in the melon's breath, and it is wet
with what you are. (I, too, ferment.)
You rub the hum and simple warmth
of summer from afar into the hips
of insects and of everything.
I can forget.
             And like the sea,
one more machine without a memory,
I don't believe that you made me.

Prime

I don't believe that you made me
into this tremolo of hands,
this fever, this flat-footed dance
of tendons and the drapery

of skin along a skeleton.
I am that I am: a brittle
ribcage and the hummingbird
of breath that flickers in it.

Incrementally, I stand:
in me are eons and the cramp
of endless ancestry.

Sun is in the leaves again.
I think I see you in the wind
but then I think I see the wind.

Terce

But then I think I see the wind
as an intention, pressing us
with weather. All the pieces
of the air you've put together
somehow know just how to hold
the rain. They somehow know

to funnel and unfold, to swerve
the snow, to rake the beaches
and to slope the arcing seagull's wings.
As wind inside a shell: they know
you in themselves. I'll find you out;
I can know you as a hint in things.

I do. And through the window
I have known you as an opening.

Sext

I have known you as an opening
of curtains as a light blurts through
the sky. But this is afternoon
and afternoon is not the time

to hunt you with the hot globe
of a human eye. So I fluster
like a crooked broom in rounds
within the living room, and try
to lift an ear to you. I try.

I cut myself into a cave for you.
To be a trilling blindness
in the infinite vibration
of your murmuring July,
I cut myself into a cave for you.

None

I cut myself into a cave for you,
but you are quiet. You are shy:

an only child, you still hide
from blame and invitations

and you constantly deny
all suitors. I will not be

defied: *you* are the tongue
I plunge into this begging

razorblade so brightened
by my spiderweb of blood,

you are the one: you are
the venom in the serpent

I have tried not to become,
my Lord. You are the one.

Vespers

My Lord, you are the one:
your breath has blown away
          the visionary sun
and now suffocates the skyline
          with a dusk. If only once,
I wish that you could shudder
with my pulse,   double over
and convulse   on the stitches
in the skin that I slash wishes in.
          But, Lord, you are the gulf
between the hoped-for
                    and the happening:
You've won.   So what is left for me
when what is left for me has come?

Compline

when what is left for me has come:
when what is left has left its wing
in something slumped against a door:

when what is left for me has come
to nothing ever after and before
this kingdom come to nothing:
when what has come is nothing more
than what was left and what was left
is nothing more than what has come
to nothing ever after and before:
if what is left is what is meant
for me and what is meant for me
is nothing come to nothing come
to this kingdom come to nothing:

Nocturne

To This Kingdom Come to Nothing:

I have itemized the night. I have held
within the livid tissue of my mouth
every particle of light and even now
I am a maze of radiation. I have felt
in each of my one hundred trillion cells
the rapturous, proud swell of darkling sounds
whose undulations break a body down
to sprays of elemental matter. As well
I have obtained a straightforward account
of the forces and conditions that propelled
the universe to burst from nothing else
and I can tell of every trembling genesis.

There is no end,

What Has Come
Will Come Again

Vigils

There is no end: what has come will come again
will come again: and then distend: and then
and then: and then again: there is no end

to origin and and: there is again
and born again: there is the forming and:
the midnight curling into morning and

the glory and again: there is no end:
there is the blessing in an and and an again:
the limitlessly yessing of began

begins incessantly again: and then
the infinite undressing of all when
there is the lifting everything again

the glowing endlessness and then
the floating endlessly again

Matins

The floating endlessly again:
the glowing and the growing back
again as I am as I can and I can stand.
I understand.
    Though I am fashioned
in the haggard image of a man,
I am an atom of the aperture.

I am as a nerve inside a gland.

I understand. Though I am fashioned
as I am, I am a perch for the eternal
and a purse for what it lends.
I understand.
    Though flakes of fire
overwhelm the fallen snow, though ice
caps melt, though oceans freeze or overflow,
somehow I am sturdier, more sure.

FINIS.

It's hard to pick a favorite from *Space, in Chains,* which is one of those books that sews itself into you, poem by poem, but the precise, evocative imagery and invitation of "Home" reckons with that most famous of odes about truth and beauty and says something entirely new. I love the motion and silence at the end of it, how it tugs you and lets you go.

MARIA HUMMEL, APR/Honickman
First Book Prize winner

Home

Laura Kasischke
Space, in Chains (2011)

It would take forever to get there
but I would know it anywhere:

My white horse grazing in my blossomy field.
Its soft nostrils. The petals
falling from the trees into the stream.

The festival would be about to begin
in the dusky village in the distance. The doe
frozen at the edge of the grove:

She leaps. She vanishes. My face—
She has taken it. And my name—

(Although the plaintive lark in the tall
grass continues to say and to say it.)

Yes. This is the place.
Where my shining treasure has been waiting.
Where my shadow washes itself in my fountain.

A few graves among the roses. Some moss
on those. An ancient

bell in a steeple down the road
making no sound at all
as the monk pulls and pulls on the rope.

On "Space, in chains" by Laura Kasischke

I love the title poem from Laura Kasischke's collection *Space, in Chains*. I'll never forget hearing Laura read it: there was this haunting energy to the poem, and at the same time it explored the themes of beauty and loss in such an unflinching way. The subject is family, but also the strangeness and chaos of life itself. And beneath it all, there's a playfulness to the language: the words "Hamster, tulips, love, gigantic squid. *To live.* I'm not endorsing it." We feel a sort of universal anxiousness about the small boy in boots as he steps out the door, perhaps the first measure of loss. And finally, when you think about it, a poem itself is a space in chains. This poem accomplishes so much. It's both dark and dazzling.

KIM BROWN SEELY, Board Member

On "Auburn Poem" by Hayden Carruth

With syntactic genius, Carruth's poems fold and unfold in subtle yet surprising ways. I've always felt Carruth was something of a Romantic realist: rooted in the knowledge and wisdom of the ills that so often define our lives but also unafraid to flirt with sentimentality, if only to give his readers the gift of relativity, dimension, and depth.

KERRY JAMES EVANS, Poet

On "Om" by Chris Abani

When I was going through the hiring process for my position at the Press—almost broke and deeply desirous to be a part of an institution I'd venerated for years, so nervous about the interviews that it felt like my teeth were vibrating—I carried my copy of *Sanctificum* with me as a talisman.

The opening sequence, "Om," sets the tone of veneration that reverberates throughout the entire book. I love how the first line invites you into Abani's memories ("The hills of my childhood are purple with dusk and wings—") and how, despite the distance from his youth and his homeland, he remains rooted there and haunted by visions of what he has seen, which seem to overlay his contemporary life like transparent photographs. In Abani's world, everything is embodied, everything is holy, whether beautiful or unspeakable, remembered or imagined.

JANEEN ARMSTRONG, Intern Program Manager and Reader Services Manager

On "Pacific" by Bob Hicok

Bob Hicok's "Pacific" takes me inside the narrator, and through him to the woman behind the desk at the hotel, and through her to the kid he is talking to, and to the kid's angry parents, and the narrator's wish to give the kid something to protect him from his parents' anger, and all of them "listening to the radio of the ocean." The poem lets me feel the lives of all these people listening to the radio of the ocean with me, wanting to "carry someone barefoot over broken glass." It does what I want a poem to do: to take me out of my little self, to go on living.

DAN GERBER, Poet

But, oh, how I can feel that cold Chicago dawn, see the faces of the musicians separated from their instruments after making them sing, the clink of their glasses as they gratefully sustain themselves with something as simple as scrambled eggs, their silence as they lean into each other, and the unsaid knowledge that any attempt to talk about what they created together would not only not suffice but also somehow diminish it. Ironically proving, once again, that words often fail us.

TINA SCHUMANN, Grant Writer and Intern

Scrambled Eggs and Whiskey

Hayden Carruth
Scrambled Eggs & Whiskey: Poems 1991–1995 (1996)

Scrambled eggs and whiskey
in the false-dawn light. Chicago,
a sweet town, bleak, God knows,
but sweet. Sometimes. And
weren't we fine tonight?
When Hank set up that limping
treble roll behind me
my horn just growled and I
thought my heart would burst.
And Brad M. pressing with the
soft stick, and Joe-Anne
singing low. Here we are now
in the White Tower, leaning
on one another, too tired
to go home. But don't say a word,
don't tell a soul, they wouldn't
understand, they couldn't, never
in a million years, how fine,
how magnificent we were
in that old club tonight.

I love this poem for the irony of the Homeric epic, the heroic.

SCOTT HIGHTOWER, Poet

Voyager
Carolyn Kizer
The Nearness of You (1986)

for Charles Gullans

I.

Digging my claws in sand, I crawled ashore.
Children stopped their play to stare. One boy
Threw me his coat, then fled. I fell asleep
Easily, on this mild, familiar strand.
Women came running, hauled me up, then clung
Like faded pennons to my broken rigging.
Homeward they lugged the light bones of my legend.

But they were weak, and stumbled in the sand . . .
Did all of you journey with me in your minds,
Aged and disabled crones? At our last parting
We tumbled in the sand, and you were bitter girls
Flinging farewells at us, like pelting stones
At a retreating army. We had seemed brilliant,
Sure of our rendezvous—but you commenced our exile.

For nightmare weeks we searched our neighbor's coast
Looking to join the force that was arrayed
To march against those traitors to the Peace.
We never heard. Did they depart without us?
Did a tidal wave obliterate the camp,
The many thousand men, the tents, the stallions,
The muscled armorers hammering at the forge?

Weapons stacked beside the saffron tents
High as the ridgepole; whole sheep on the spits
Sputtering fat that flared the fires for miles;
Camp-sounds: the creak of leather saddles, hooves
On hard-packed ground, men's curses, yapping dogs.
The cold soft voice of that great General:
Did he burn or drown? Is he in hiding now?

Wine of my province! Tasting it again
I taste my own blood, sweet when I sucked a scratch
In boyhood. Yet the aftertaste is sour,
Spoilt by an old man's breath, death in his throat.
And now I spill the cup. My hands are stiff
As a galley-slave's, and split from brine and rowing,
Smooth when I left, commander of the fleet.

II.

I gave the orders that we must abandon
The search for armies that abandoned us.
Like hounds grown lean from looking, we raced back
Across the fastest, brightest autumn sea!
Sights were inaccurate: one long ribbon beach
A long mirage, seducing us from the North,
Our true direction, toward a curving bay

Shaped like a siren's mouth. The Navigator
Hunted our home beyond another cove
So like the one we turned to all our lives
We feared that Heaven's hand had scooped you up,
Moved huts and livestock, children's prints in sand
Clean from the place, and set you down on grass
And daisies, in pale meadows of the dead.

We disembarked to search those teasing hills
Whose contours were familiar as our wives'.
But gradually the verdure of the slopes
Turned tropical, and we were jungle-bound.
A bird screamed like a brother; near the ground
A deadly, chuckling voice from ferns and moss.
Roots toiled our feet like snakes, became snakes.

All life voracious, fearsome, ravenous!
Great orchids dipped and gulped: and soldiers vanished
Silently, where they stood. Only the clang
Of a dropped shield on a log, or the soft hinge
Of closing flower jaws ... we could not tell.
A few pulled back in time, but never whole.
As we wallowed on, we smelled our rot.

The rain descended, not quick jungle storms
But seas upended. And the land joined in,
All elements reversing: skies dropped mud
Like excrements of Gods ... and we, whipped blind

And putrid, fled to the immaculate sea.
So we believed. Staggering, caked like apes
With soil, we sensed the rains' diminishing.

Still we were puppets to the dirt. We whirled
Choking in storms of all the vast world's dust.
How many last words strangled in a cough?
We fell to the ground, to join our dust to dust.
The breeze turned sweet and whistled us awake.
We rose like the dead in vestments of white dust
But could not praise the landscape. There was none.

Only the land we stood on, like the deck
Of the universe, lost in seas of vacant space;
Laughing, with barren minds and eyes, we stared:
Scarecrow confronting scarecrow in a field
Banging our arms against our smoking sides.
And so we danced like grains of emery
Polishing the round lens of the world.

        III.

The Navigator fumbled at a rag
Which was a map, its rivers silted up.
We followed him, till, drowning in the sand,
He said he needed water under him
To chase the stars that wriggled in the sky
Like jellyfish. But with his closing eyes
He sighted spars, or trees, or picks for teeth . . .

Perspective lied: a camel was a cat.
But, singing folly and mad hope aloud,
He died too soon. For if we hadn't killed him
We could have cursed him as we dragged him up
To scrape his snout over the rotten planking
Of the one remaining ship, her side stove in,
And knock his bones across that broken deck.

Despair turned lyric, and we moved like dancers:
One man fingered a rusty nail, another
Sifted a cornucopia of wheatlike sand
That overflowed the hold, and lay there humming.
For weeks, unlaboring, we watched the season alter,
Till winter fell on us like crashing armor
And the living used the dead for food and shelter.

In Spring a friendly caïque picked us up.
We voyaged from isle to isle, all so alike
I could repeat one story for all. No doubt I will,
The gaffer huddled in his moldy corner,
A bore to his descendants, mouthing lies.
So now you face the Hero, breath to breath,
And know no more than he what victory was.

I love this poem because of the multiple voices and turns it inhabits. The landscape becomes part of the humans, and their stories wander like minds, roads, or water. It is an expert stroke of form and image and meaning coming together in that quirky, surprising voice that could only be Perillo's.

JEREMY VOIGT, Website Proofreader
and Intern

Driving Home from the Conference like a Pill with a Thousand People Inside

Lucia Perillo
Inseminating the Elephant (2009)

We turned off the highway at Chuckanut Drive
(everyone told us to turn off at Chuckanut Drive)
where, when we finally slid from the cedars,
the ocean smacked us in the face.
Jane squints down into her steering and talking
(her voice like the *hushing* of the wet road)
about how her mother fled from the house
(one of the many times he beat her).
How they wore their pajamas into the store
after crossing the parking-lot stripes in their slippers—
see how easy it is to start over
after the hangers screech.
In the motel, there'd always be a picture of the sea
(as if all you needed was the *idea* of its rocking)—
you feel your life starting over on Chuckanut Drive
(is what made Jane remember).
Our car crept like a grub on the country's edge,
there on a cliff above Samish Bay:
mountains to the north, mountains to the south,
(& a life equaled)
the huge unbroken water in between.

Full disclosure: Lucia Perillo was a beloved friend. Among her many, many poems, "The Second Slaughter" is the one I return to most. I recall first reading it one bleak day in *Poetry* magazine before it appeared in *On the Spectrum of Possible Deaths.* It's pure Lucia: narrative and lyric, conveyed by hard fact, then lifted into myth. Bits from *The Iliad* remind us how ancient it is, violence—and rage, revenge—and how even grief can be unspeakably brutal. It goes beyond sorrow, every human gene deep. You can't look away.

The penultimate stanza, its recent history, I see so clearly—the burning Persian oil wells, tar "weighting" the feathers as birds "dragged through black shallows." Trained as a natural historian and forester, Lucia zoom-lenses into their feathers, their terrible fate. But the ending seven lines floor me; I will never get over them. *Inhuman* paired with *lament,* the starving jackal with the speaker, the word *posture* surely nowhere else so loaded and layered and bent low and triumphant. And the shocking double take of that "looks like appeasement / though it is not."

No, it is not. Thus poetry.

MARIANNE BORUCH, Poet

The Second Slaughter

Lucia Perillo
On the Spectrum of Possible Deaths (2012)

Achilles slays the man who slew his friend, pierces the corpse
behind the heels and drags it
behind his chariot like the cans that trail
a bride and groom. Then he lays out
a banquet for his men, oxen and goats
and pigs and sheep; the soldiers eat
until a greasy moonbeam lights their beards.

The first slaughter is for victory, but the second slaughter is for grief—
in the morning more animals must be killed
for burning with the body of the friend. But Achilles finds
no consolation in the hiss and crackle of their fat;
not even heaving four stallions on the pyre
can lift the ballast of his sorrow.

And here I turn my back on the epic hero—the one who slits
the throats of his friend's dogs,
killing what the loved one loved
to reverse the polarity of grief. Let him repent
by vanishing from my concern
after he throws the dogs onto the fire.
The singed fur makes the air too difficult to breathe.

When the oil wells of Persia burned I did not weep
until I heard about the birds, the long-legged ones especially
which I imagined to be scarlet, with crests like egrets
and tails like peacocks, covered in tar
weighting the feathers they dragged through black shallows
at the rim of the marsh. But once

I told this to a man who said I was inhuman, for giving animals
my first lament. So now I guard
my inhumanity like the jackal
who appears behind the army base at dusk,
come there for scraps with his head lowered
in a posture that looks like appeasement
though it is not.

On "Hide-and-Seek with God" by Brenda Shaughnessy

I love Brenda Shaughnessy's "Hide-and-Seek with God" for its imagined, or perhaps enacted, engagement with an all-powerful, immensely threatening Divine and how that engagement interweaves with a profoundly personal story.

ALICIA JO RABINS, Poet

On "God of rooms" by Jean Valentine

I encountered both Jean Valentine's "God of rooms" and the collection it comes from while at Copper Canyon Press. The poem is a mere eight lines, but muscly, weird, and beautiful at all points. Valentine's work, I think, represents the Press's commitment to voices that are as powerful as they are subtle.

SAM ROBISON, Intern

On *Letter to an Imaginary Friend* by Thomas McGrath

Letter to an Imaginary Friend is probably the best of many attempts at America's epic poem.

ROGER MITCHELL, Poet

On "Frottage" by Dean Young

Dean Young's "Frottage" remains one of the most original and impressive feats of craft I've encountered in American poetry. It was one of the first poems I ever read by Dean Young so many years ago, and it remains vital to my own thinking about and teaching of poetry.

JASWINDER BOLINA, Poet

The leaps of imagination in this poem startled me at first, the way that, reading, I felt myself transported inside the mind of a frenetic, hyperactive thinker, one who can move from an obliterated moon to an ornamental surfboard in just a few lines. It wasn't until I reached the end, though, that I realized the true seriousness of this poem—that rectangle of darkness that "approacheth on wheelchair wheels." What is that? Death? Obliteration? Loss? And are the critics of the title merely those who would criticize Young's own poetry? (The poem appears on the back of his book, where blurbs would normally be, after all.) Or are they more powerful? Are they cultural memory? Legacy? God?

KEVIN PRUFER, Poet

To the Critics

Dean Young
Shock by Shock (2015)

My helmet is almost done
and when it is I will hurtle
through outer space until you won't
be able to differentiate me from
any other celestial debris so
you will have to respect me
because I could obliterate your moon
so there'd be no tides
and your surfboard would become
even more ornamental although
you'd still have your orange kayak.
In the '70s, *Kayak* was a great
poetry magazine, editor George Hitchcock.
People have woefully lost touch
with the surreal pirate-radio signal
of their own hearts but not everyone
is dead! Have you ever tried
to stand up on a bicycle?
Have you ever tried to stand up
on a bicycle juggling lemons?
Have you ever tried to stand up
on a bicycle made of glass
juggling lemon trees while
a huge rectangle of darkness
approacheth on wheelchair wheels?
Sure you have.

This poem holds us suspended in a solitude we can feel. In lonely fragments, the persona aches and echoes after *you*. It's enough to stop you cold.

CLARETTA HOLSEY, Production Editor
and Intern

Solitude Is a Winter before the Sea of the Past
Fernando Valverde, translated from the Spanish by Carolyn Forché
America (2021)

The beach is lonely,
there is a gap between the years,
it was yesterday,
I was lying there,
there came familiar voices
that woke me up,
but nobody was there anymore,
then I wanted
to walk in their footsteps,
pursue those voices
that did not make a sound
but which were
sounding
inside my ears,
within my concern
and I walked,
I walked hardly stopping
until I saw myself
in the middle of a lonely beach,
empty,
just before
getting into the sea
chasing some voices,
just before,
absence,
from the sea,
of you.

This little poem behaves like a Li Po poem leaping out of ninth-century China across time and into our contemporary lives, affirming the precarious power of poetry.

JOHN BALABAN, Poet and Translator

Festival

Joseph Stroud
Of This World: New and Selected Poems 1966–2006 (2008)

We are at the gate above the river.
Peach trees surround the pavilion.
It is the time of the Emperor's feast,
the bounty of his riches and exquisite ladies.
Over there is Li Po, drunk and sick
on rice wine. They unscroll the silk
before him. The crowd is quiet. Error
is not allowed. Li Po has to be held,
the brush shakes in his hand. Suddenly
the poem lurches out. A sword in sunlight.
Our broken machine of language at last
at flow with the river. Fireworks
and sparklers cast lights on the water.
Lamps are lit on the fragile trees.
Do you see the Emperor, abandoned and alone,
in the crowd of weeping faces?

✐ Here, humor meets transcendence.

MICHAEL WIEGERS, Executive Editor

Complaining about Losing My Hair
Pai Chu-yi, translated from the Chinese by Red Pine
Finding Them Gone: Visiting China's Poets of the Past (2016)

I complained about losing my hair in the morning
I complained about losing my hair at night
once it was gone I complained even more
but once it was gone wasn't so bad
no need to wash it or rinse it
no need to comb it or tie it
perfectly fine in the sun or rain
my head with no topknot felt light
and once I took off my dirt-covered cap
and untied my dusty hatstrings
and filled a silver vase with cold water
and poured it over my crown
anointing myself with fine oil it seemed
I suddenly felt cool and refreshed
now I know why those carefree monks
avail themselves of a shave

I have always loved the elegance of the cover of Alfred Corn's *Contradictions*, which features a beautiful Agnes Martin image and suggests a poet of vivid grace, control, and subtlety. (The image, however, doesn't accommodate Corn's wicked sense of humor.) His classic book *The Poem's Heartbeat* is a master class in prosody.

MICHAEL WIEGERS, Executive Editor

The Common Thread

Alfred Corn
Contradictions (2008)

In the graphic textiles of experience,
Where themes are threads, trace the one that runs,
First, through the fable of the compliant Cat
Who combed red coals (the Monkey goading, scolding)
To rake out toasted chestnuts tittering guile
Could then with unharmed fingers peel and eat,
Not one left for the dupe who scorched her paw;
That, and the clemency of Coriolanus,
Sparing ancestral Rome a bloody sack,
His banishment, meanwhile, still not rescinded;
And the French maxim noting that we all
Have fortitude enough to endure the torment
Of persons not ourselves; or gibes lobbed at
The man forsaken: "Others he saved, himself
He cannot save."
                        Like common thread, serene
Expedience outstrips the speed of insight,
Consolidating patches of a quilt
To keep complacency snug as toast—for instance,
The donors who, instead of food or shelter,
Sent cast-off, threadbare T-shirts to survivors
Of the hurricane, a few with printed slogans,
Home truths like, "Life's a bitch, and then you die."

It's wonderful to consider ekphrastic poetry, and Forrest Gander's interactions with the photos of Jack Shear in *Knot* are spectacular examples of the endeavor. In the final photograph of that collection, Shear offers a startling permutation of the body-and-cloak theme of the book: the figure in apparent free fall, the cloak whipping upward in flame-like turbulence, obscuring him entirely save two arms in desperate reaches on either side. With a sinister omniscience, Gander fingers the "you" of this figure as though sentencing him: "In a dark / seam of disturbance / you suck hard for any air / the fire hasn't eaten." The poem mimics both fire and a descent into hell, and with subtle nods to Dante (the greatest sin that of betraying "the heart of the one / who loved you most") as well as Eurydice and Lot's Wife (both punished for "glancing / back over your shoulder.")

Gander interacts with powerful emotions of guilt and anguish. Most astonishing, however, are his final lines, which swiftly neuter all emotional experience with an existential tautology: "are / and are not." This poem, while macabre and even disturbing, illuminates how vulnerable we are as humans, how our guilt proves the strength of our care, what we wish we could have done.

RYO YAMAGUCHI, Publicist

"The speech balloon"

Forrest Gander
Knot (2022)

The speech balloon
has gone missing, but still
the silence crackles. In a dark
seam of disturbance
you suck hard for any air
the fire hasn't eaten.
Your arms flap from your
vanishing point. Your
mind in the updraft,
smoke rises in your throat.
Kindness and daylight
will outlive you, but what
did you ever have to do
with either? You, who
poked the tunneling
larva of disappointment
into a hairline crack
in the heart of the one
who loved you most. You

can't be surprised, glancing
back over your shoulder now,
eyes wide, pupils
dilated, at the wake of
unmanageable pain, the
devastation. And because your words
carried so much weight,
the given length of your
time here
has snapped off prematurely.
Cauterized, thrust into this
torrent of heat
you are
and are not.

"Lament" is an angry, tender poem about the impending loss of the speaker's mother. Oedipal, it's told in a voice that might be a lover's. Is the lament the mother's because she has only these slick, nearly bare branches of the budding cherry tree to pull against her breast, not a child, not a husband? Or is it the son's lament, seeing his mother bereft, pained because she is leaving him as well as her life?

ELAINE TERRANOVA, Poet

Lament

Stephen Berg
New & Selected Poems (1992)

My mother wants to be burned, she told me
last night stretched out watching TV
after I told her what the doctor said.
"Don't put me anywhere, either," she added.
I left the room, came back
and found her leaning out a window,
fondling, whispering to the slick branches
of the cherry tree, freshly budded,
shiny after rain,
that brushed the front of my house,
pulling them against her naked breasts
to soothe herself with the cool leafy wood,
to feel something other than her own hands
touch the nipples.

Stories from Our House

Dear friends,
    I recently discovered the ~~notebook I~~
kept as an intern: "Being at CCP has taught
me about passion for what you do, working
hard and seeing your labor on bookshelves
and how much that means. It's shown
me collaboration and communication are
everything in the creation of work we
can all love.
    "I'd rather
    burn myself down
    than change the locks."
        - Rachel McKibbens, 'Letter from my
        Brain to my Heart'
            - blvd
All my love,
            EMMy

Copper Canyon Press
Come shining Project
PO Box 271
Port Townsend, WA
98368

One day, Sam Hamill wrote to me out of the blue, and said he'd like to be my publisher. Joy! Since then, I've done four books with CCP. But my relationship with the Press is far deeper than that. When I became ill in 2008, CCP acquired Ausable Press, the small poetry press I had founded ten years earlier. So both I and my poets now have the best possible home. Chase Twichell

Why "Twigs"? Because it is beautiful and, like all Taha's work, puts a human hand to history. Because "art is worthless / unless it plants / a measure of splendor in people's hearts." Because Taha recited it to me in Nazareth in 2007 and wrote an inscription in Arabic: "Dear Jeff, Welcome to our house."

JEFFREY BROWN, Poet

Taha Muhammad Ali came to my home with Peter Cole and, for the first time, I heard Arabic aloud in words of poetry. The ancient sounds washed over me as Taha read in Arabic and then Peter translated his work into English. I felt like I woke to a hidden love, a music kept from me.

SARAH CAVANAUGH, Board Member

Taha Muhammad Ali's "Twigs" was one of the first poems I read by a Copper Canyon poet. I was in South Africa and intensely intrigued by this poetry-only publisher in the United States that was publishing a Palestinian poet with English translations alongside the original Arabic. Who was this publisher? I had to know. This was one of the factors that led to my role as an intern with the Press in 2007, then as the editor of *Push Open the Window* (2011), and now, back in South Africa, as one of the Press's copyeditors.

I will always be grateful to Taha for this poem and for leading me to Copper Canyon. I have the framed broadside in my living room, where it reminds me every day "that water is the finest drink, / and bread the most delicious food, / and that art is worthless / unless it plants / a measure of splendor in people's hearts."

ALISON LOCKHART, Copyeditor, Proofreader, and Intern

Twigs

Taha Muhammad Ali, translated from the Arabic
by Peter Cole, Yahya Hijazi, and Gabriel Levin
So What: New & Selected Poems (with a story), 1971–2005 (2006)

Neither music,
fame, nor wealth,
not even poetry itself,
could provide consolation
for life's brevity,
or the fact that *King Lear*
is a mere eighty pages long and comes to an end,
and for the thought that one might suffer greatly
on account of a rebellious child.

~

My love for you
is what's magnificent,
but I, you, and the others,
most likely,
are ordinary people.

~

My poem
goes beyond poetry
because you
exist
beyond the realm of women.

~

And so
it has taken me
all of sixty years
to understand
that water is the finest drink,
and bread the most delicious food,
and that art is worthless
unless it plants
a measure of splendor in people's hearts.

~

After we die,
and the weary heart
has lowered its final eyelid
on all that we've done,
and on all that we've longed for,
on all that we've dreamt of,
all we've desired
or felt,
hate will be
the first thing
to putrefy
within us.

1989–91

Seeing that Copper Canyon Press published *King Me* made me want to become a Copper Canyon poet, either via a debut collection or a later book. Thankfully, things worked out for me on the debut front.

JACOB SAENZ, APR/Honickman First Book Prize winner

Some Young Kings

Roger Reeves
King Me (2013)

The Mike Tyson in me sings like a narwhal
minus the nasally twang of sleeping in a cold ocean,
the unsightly barnacles latched to the mattress
of skin just below my eye, the white horn
jutting out from the top of my head—
oh god bless us mutts—the basset-blood-
hound mulattoes, the pug-mixed puppies
left behind the dog pound's cinder-block walls
as German shepherds, Labradoodles,
and Portuguese water dogs turn their inbred behinds
and narrow backs at our small-mouthed blues.
It's hard to smile with an ear in your mouth,
two names, and a daughter hanging by a thread
from the railing of a treadmill. Oh neck
and North Carolina and a white coat of paint
for all the faces of my Negro friends
hanging from trees in Salisbury.
Greensboro. And Guilford County.
The hummingbirds inside my chest,
with their needle-nose pliers for tongues
and hammer-heavy wings, have left a mess
of ticks in my lungs and a punctured lullaby
in my throat. Little boy blue come blow
your horn. The cow's in the meadow.
And Dorothy's alone in the corn with Jack,
his black fingers, the brass of his lips,
the half-moons of his fingernails clicking
along her legs until she howls—
Charlie Parker. Charlie Parker. Charlie Parker.
Oz is a man with a mute body
on an HBO original show that I am too afraid to watch
for fear of finding my uncle,
or a man that looks like my uncle,
which means finding a man that looks like me

in another man's embrace or slumped over a shiv
made from a mattress coil and a bar of Ivory soap.
Most young kings return home without their heads.
It's 1941, and Jack Johnson still loves white women,
and my mother won't forgive him.
If she can't use your comb, don't bring her home,
my mother says in 1998. It's 2009,
and I still love white women.
Charlie Parker. Charlie Parker. Charlie Parker.
Often, I click the heels of my Nikes together
when talking to the police, I am a cricket
crushed beneath a car's balding black tires.
Most young kings return home without their heads.

Recommended by **MICHAEL WIEGERS**, Executive Editor

Evolution of My Block

Jacob Saenz
Throwing the Crown (2018)

As a boy I bicycled the block
w/a brown mop top falling
into a tail bleached blond,

gold-like under golden light,
like colors of Noble Knights
'banging on corners, unconcerned

w/the colors I bore—a shorty
too small to war with, too brown
to be down for the block.

White Knights became brown
Kings still showing black & gold
on corners now crowned,

the block a branch branded
w/la corona graffitied on
garage doors by the pawns.

As a teen, I could've beamed
the crown, walked in w/out
the beat down custom,

warred w/my cousin
who claimed Two-Six,
the set on the next block

decked in black & beige.
But I preferred games to gangs,
books to crooks wearing hats

crooked to the left or right
fighting for a plot, a block
to spot & mark w/blood

of boys who knew no better
way to grow up than throw up
the crown & be down for whatever.

The package of Copper Canyon books that arrives regularly for me is an extraordinary gift, as has been the opportunity to work with Copper Canyon Press. It changed my life.

ELIZABETH J. COLEMAN, Editor of *Here: Poems for the Planet* (2019)

On *13th Balloon* by Mark Bibbins

I first met Mark Bibbins when he called me to tell me that I'd been accepted to The New School's MFA program. I've since grown to know him as an excellent educator, fierce advocate of poetry, and truly beautiful poet. The excerpt on pages 9 and 10 from his book-length poem, *13th Balloon,* made me cry the first time I read it. Mark can write about loss with so much love and grace and humor and care. Working on this book with Mark was one of the highlights of my time at Copper Canyon Press.

LAURA BUCCIERI, Director of Publicity

On "Travelers" by Ursula K. Le Guin

I chose this poem from Ursula K. Le Guin's *So Far So Good,* completed shortly before her death in 2018, because of its simplicity and humility. Even though Le Guin was most celebrated for her science fiction novels, she began as a poet. I love her unflinching meditations on mortality and mystery in this final collection, as well as the references to the timeless beauty of the Pacific Northwest— its wind and mist and rock and light. Also, I had the great honor of reading this manuscript when Le Guin first submitted it. I imagined the legendary author hitting Send. She died exactly one week after I received it. This is her farewell. It is a gem and reminds me that we are all in this together.

KIM BROWN SEELY, Board Member

On "These Poems" by June Jordan

One of the most meaningful projects I worked on at Copper Canyon Press was *The Essential June Jordan*. I love this poem from June Jordan's work because it invites us in, not just to her poems but to the ethos of Copper Canyon Press widely.

PETER SZILAGYI, Intern

My first involvement with Copper Canyon was in 2018, when I read at the release party for Ursula K. Le Guin's collection *So Far So Good* at Hugo House. It was my first year as Seattle's Youth Poet Laureate and one of my first readings outside of a spoken-word space. I felt nervous and exhilarated standing on that stage, occupying the same space where Ursula would have read from. Afterward, Elaina Ellis congratulated me and gave me five books, all of which have moved with me to three different cities.

Four years later, I got to be an intern for the Press that helped welcome me into poetry. I'm so thankful to have made even a small impact on the future of the Press, for Copper Canyon has impacted me so much. I'll carry that gratitude wherever I go.

AZURA TYABJI, Intern

To the Rain

Ursula K. Le Guin
So Far So Good: Final Poems: 2014–2018 (2018)

Mother rain, manifold, measureless,
falling on fallow, on field and forest,
on house-roof, low hovel, high tower,
downwelling waters all-washing, wider
than cities, softer than sisterhood, vaster
than countrysides, calming, recalling:
return to us, teaching our troubled
souls in your ceaseless descent
to fall, to be fellow, to feel to the root,
to sink in, to heal, to sweeten the sea.

One day Michael Wiegers came in holding a new manuscript. "Are any of you fans of Ursula Le Guin?" he asked us interns. My hand shot up. I grew up reading her novels, many of them meaning a great deal to me. "Well, do you want to read her new book?"

"Leaves" is a quiet, humble, and reflective piece. Le Guin looks back on her life as a flicker. Am I that person? What brought me here? What will stay behind? When I read this poem, I am able to think back fondly on my time at Copper Canyon Press and to look forward to whatever comes next.

JACOB BOLES, Intern

Leaves

Ursula K. Le Guin
So Far So Good: Final Poems: 2014–2018 (2018)

Years do odd things to identity.
What does it mean to say
I am that child in the photograph
at Kishamish in 1935?
Might as well say I am the shadow
of a leaf of the acacia tree
felled seventy years ago
moving on the page the child reads.
Might as well say I am the words she read
or the words I wrote in other years,
flicker of shade and sunlight
as the wind moves through the leaves.

I happened upon this poem while doing some research during my Copper Canyon internship, and I immediately felt connected to it. It will always hold for me, within its own images, the feeling of Port Townsend, the desks we gathered together, the smell of tea brewing, and the little resident spider we named sitting behind the printer.

HANNAH MESSINGER, Intern

The New Savagery

Dean Young
Bender: New & Selected Poems (2012)

What does the new savagery
require of me? If I pound a nail
into the wall, the wall is my heart.
All that gnawing on my own headbone—

that was the old savagery, a lassitudinous
charade, black leather jacket boom boom
long after the sun had set and all
that was left was for the dancers
to put their clothes back on.

The mind twists its silver wire.
A tiny mechanical bird is made to sing.

I will write another long last letter
about what I had for lunch, what had me
and you will understand my feelings,
how they only want to feel yours

and if the duty of my dejections
takes me into the sky, no one
must follow me. Not mother
made of balsa wood, not father,
the plinth. Even you, my love,
must not get covered with that ash.

Why am I so afraid of nothingness?
My soul is a baby wolf.

I was living in the Northwest when I first read—and then met—Kizer. She was the same person in person as she was in print. I was directing the literature programs for Centrum in Port Townsend in the late 1970s and had her teach one of the summer workshops. To put it mildly, none of the other distinguished instructors upstaged her.

JIM HEYNEN, Poet

from "Pro Femina"

Carolyn Kizer
Cool, Calm & Collected: Poems 1960–2000 (2002)

While men have politely debated free will, we have howled for it.
Howl still, pacing the centuries, tragedy heroines.
Some who sat quietly in the corner with their embroidery
Were Defarges, stabbing the wool with the names of their ancient
Oppressors, who ruled by the divine right of the male—
I'm impatient of interruptions! I'm aware there were millions
Of mutes for every Saint Joan or sainted Jane Austen,
Who, vague-eyed and acquiescent, worshiped God as a man.
I'm not concerned with those cabbageheads, not truly feminine
But neutered by labor. I mean real women, like *you* and like *me*.

On "Rain Light" by W.S. Merwin

The first time I heard William read, I was transfixed by "The Last One." I then had the honor of serving on the Copper Canyon Press board and the founding board of the Merwin Conservancy. "Rain Light" was the last poem I heard him recite by heart. Even when his memory began to fail him, these words remained.

SARAH CAVANAUGH, Board Member

It's a dream, but true: We stood in the midst of the palm forest—William, me, his Paula, and mine—and he recited "Rain Light."

JEFFREY BROWN, Poet

On "Vixen" by W.S. Merwin

Several years ago, William and I were walking in a forest near Sun Valley, Idaho. I mentioned how open and light-filled the woods were compared to those surrounding my home near Seattle. Suddenly, something rushed across the trail about forty yards in front of us. William was looking down and didn't see it, but wanted to know everything—its shape, height, color, and speed. I thought of his words in "Vixen" as we walked there and many times since: "Comet of stillness princess of what is over . . . let me catch sight of you again."

LINDA BIERDS, Poet

On "Note" by W.S. Merwin

I was privileged to share many spotlight moments with William because of my Copper Canyon Press and Merwin Conservancy board service. But the most meaningful time we shared was in his quiet Haiku home as we discussed his legacy project. Mindful of my service for his publisher and conservancy, he asked if there was anything he could do for me in gratitude. That moment was a gift, I said, "an ineffable note etched in my memory." With that, he handwrote his poem "Note," and gave it to me.

JOSEPH C. ROBERTS, Board Member

Note

Remember how the naked soul
comes to language and at once knows
loss and distance and believing

then for a time it will not run
with its old freedom
like a light innocent of measure
but will hearken to how
one story becomes another
and will try to tell where
they have emerged from
and where they are heading
as though they were its own legend
running before the words and beyond them
naked and never looking back

through the noise of questions

William — for Joe, with
on Maui, April 3, 2011
affection —

[Above] "Note" written by W.S. Merwin

[Following Page] Image of Merwin's signature from Dan Waggoner's copy of "Gray Herons in the Field above the River"

When I first joined the board, Merwin won the Pulitzer. When he visited Seattle, he signed this poem for me and drew a picture of a bird next to his signature. I love the poem and the feeling it gives me. It reminds me somehow of the Skagit River.

DAN WAGGONER, Board Member

Gray Herons in the Field above the River

W.S. Merwin
The Shadow of Sirius (2008)

Now that the nights turn longer than the days
we are standing in the still light after dawn

in the high grass of autumn that is green again
hushed in its own place after the burn of summer

each of us stationed alone without moving
at a perfect distance from all the others

like shadows of ourselves risen out of our shadows
each eye without turning continues to behold

what is moving
each of us is one of seven now

we have come a long way sailing our opened clouds
remembering all night where the world would be

the clear shallow stream the leaves floating along it
the dew in the hushed field the only morning

W.S. Merwin
Feb 5 2010
Seattle

Merwin is a lighthouse poet for me—for noticing gardens, foliage, and all their inhabitants, and for reminding us that we are never alone; we are all connected.

AIMEE NEZHUKUMATATHIL, Poet

The Scarab Questions

W.S. Merwin
Garden Time (2016)

Out of full shadow your sound emerges
at the end of the last morning in May
as we call the days on our calendars
but where did you begin without numbers
where did you come from this late morning
what do you remember as you ride your one note
on its dark sunbeam out into the daylight
your note is the time of your radiance
arriving once just as the sun does
but where were you before now where did you
come from before you were today

Ethan Evans, another intern at the Press, read this poem out loud at one of our meetings, and it entirely transformed the poem for me. I would have completely missed it otherwise! Ethan read it with such energy and joy that it's one of my favorite memories from Copper Canyon Press, all of us laughing at the cleverness of the poem and Ethan's liveliness in reading it for us.

HEATHER BRENNAN, Intern

One-Star Reviews of the Taj Mahal
Aimee Nezhukumatathil
Oceanic (2018)

a found poem

Too bad it was man-made.
As a stand-alone attraction I guess it's passable
but compared to the McDonald's at Celebration Mall
it's just meh.

Not for Indians. Very tacky.

There was no cloakroom at the South Gate!

The garden is also very basic. Everything is basic.

We were ripped off by asking local shopkeepers to hold our bags for us.
You will be swarmed, swarmed by street vendors and children swarmed by
camels and parking lot goons and children and cheat cameramen and stalker
tourist guides and camel children and footwear thieves, so: MIND YOUR
BELONGINGS!

It's just an old love story.

But is it love or hate?

I was told to get out with my selfie stick!

Don't even think about seeing it under a full moon.

Can you believe this tomb has no rides?

On "Not to Be Dwelled On" by Heather McHugh

I read this first in *Poetry* magazine, in the unlikely setting of my medical clinic in Denver; I haven't seen an issue of *Poetry* in any other waiting area ever. I'd had no idea I would read it again, in manuscript, in Heather's *Upgraded to Serious*. My very first favorite poem of the year, which bestowal hadn't before occurred to me. It's the humility, baby.

DAVID CALIGIURI, Copyeditor and Proofreader

On "On Being Asked to Write a Poem Against the War in Vietnam" by Hayden Carruth

Carruth must have been quite a character. Two poet friends of mine knew him and have high regard for him: Wendell Berry and Brooks Haxton. Carruth farmed, among his other duties. When war confronts those who keep the earth, maintaining it and earning their life from it, the purpose or point of war dwindles and ceases to have any relevance. Carruth seems to have lived this trajectory—a clash of political ambition with a more humble, human effort. That clash can generate poetry, as I think it did for Carruth.

MAURICE MANNING, Poet

My love of letterforms and poetry joined the day Sam Hamill agreed to bring me on as a book designer. My life filled with poems and poets: with finding a typeface to fit a poet's voice; with building relationships in marginal discussions as we weighed the depth of indents, "oh" vs. "O," and whether set punctuation was italicized or not. Jim Harrison drew his one-eyed doodle. Merwin's handwriting was inscrutable. C.D. Wright's poetry did not fit the boundaries of standard book trim sizes.

What endures beyond my margins: Copper Canyon Press gave me women poets. The poetry canon I received in my late-1970s education was parched. Copper Canyon Press brought me to Anna Swir, C.D. Wright, Coral Bracho, Laura Kasischke, Ruth Stone, Jean Valentine, Marianne Boruch, Ellen Bass, and Natalie Scenters-Zapico, just to name some of my favorites. It is really impossible to measure that positive contribution to our world.

VALERIE BREWSTER CALDWELL, Book and Collateral Designer

Lucia was one of my favorite poets going into Copper Canyon Press, and it was one of my greatest pleasures to work with her. As a single mom new to Port Townsend, I sat many a time in the "freak-out's throne."

TONAYA ROSENBERG, Managing Editor

Freak-Out
Lucia Perillo
On the Spectrum of Possible Deaths (2012)

Mine have occurred in empty houses
down whose dark paneling I dragged my fingernails—

though big-box stores have also played their parts,
as well as entrances to indistinct commercial buildings,

cubes of space between glass yellowing like onion skin,
making my freak-out obscure.

~

Suddenly the head is being held between the hands
arranged in one of the conventional configurations:

hands on ears or hands on eyes
or both stacked on the forehead

as if to squeeze the wailing out,
as if the head were being juiced.

~

The freak-out wants wide open space,
though the rules call for containment—

there are the genuine police to be considered,
which is why I recommend the empty vestibule

though there is something to be said for freaking-out
if the meadow is willing to have you

facedown in it,
mouth open to the dry summer dirt.

~

When my friend was freaking-out inside my car, I said
she was sitting in the freak-out's throne,

which is love's throne, too, so many fluids
from within the body on display

outside the body until the chin gleams
like the extended shy head of a snail! Even

without streetlamps, even in the purplish
penumbra of the candelabra of the firs.

~

My friend was freaking-out about her freak-outs,
which happened in the produce aisle;

I said: oh yeah at night, it's very
freak-inducing when the fluorescent lights

arrest you to make their interrogation! Asking
why you can't be more like the cabbages,

stacked precariously
yet so cool and self-contained,

or like the peppers who go through life
untroubled by their freaky whorls.

~

What passes through the distillery of anguish
is the tear without the sting of salt—dripping

to fill the test tube of the body
not with monster potion but the H Two . . . oh, forget it . . .

that comes when the self is spent.
How many battles would remain

in the fetal pose if the men who rule would rip
their wool suits from their chests like girls

in olden Greece? If the bomberesses
stopped to lay their brows down on a melon.

If the torturer would only
beat the dashboard with his fists.

⌐ "Coming home" is such a beautiful poem. I always think of it after snowfall in Port Townsend.

> a voice calling us,
> reminding us there is something that is
> more even than life. Silence. Beauty.

Those lines—they pull me in continuously.

CATHERINE EDWARDS, Board
Member

Coming home

Jaan Kaplinski, translated from the Estonian
by the author with Sam Hamill and Riina Tamm
The Wandering Border (1987)

Coming home.
Three kilometers along the bank of the frozen river.
Only some open spots left.
Dozens of ducks quacking, swimming, splashing,
diving their heads into the icy water
and shaking them.
Some people standing on the bridge,
throwing them crumbs of bread.
Some lanterns in the dusk
and snow falling falling
silently, softly, and in this silence
suddenly a voice calling us,
reminding us there is something that is
more even than life. Silence. Beauty.
Falling snow. Perfect crystals. Flakes.
Harmony. Beauty. *To kalon.*
Snowflakes become drops of water
on my face. In my beard.
Sound of water buried, shut
in the silence of snow. Voice
of God. More even than God.
Snowflakes. Voice of Water. *Mizu no oto.*
Vox aquae. Vox Dei.

Larger than life—and the average airplane seat—Jim Harrison was known for a time as, perhaps, the only author on book tour who refused nonstop flights. He demanded as many short, connecting flights as possible to get wherever he was going. There was smoking, and drinking, to be done with each stop. And that he did, with gusto.

Harrison's embrace of a gout-inducing diet the Sun King could only aspire to, was in keeping with his big, American, soul-searching quest to fall from innocence as fully as one could. That legendary fall is chronicled throughout the most mind-bogglingly versatile backlist I know.

IRA SILVERBERG, Board Member

from "After Ikkyū"

Jim Harrison
The Shape of the Journey: New and Collected Poems (1998)

19

Time gets foreshortened late at night.
Jesus died a few days ago, my father
and sister just before lunch. At dawn
I fished, then hoed corn. Married at midmorning,
wept for a second. We were poor momentarily
for a decade. Within a few minutes I made
a round trip to Paris. I drank and ate during a parade
in my room. One blink, Red Mountain's still there.

On "Death Again" by Jim Harrison

In 2011, Jim Harrison's "Death Again" was read aloud several times on a trip to China with Bill Porter, Walter Parsons, Jim Wickwire, Joseph Roberts, and Jerry Fulks. It was full poetry immersion—we were constantly reading to each other and visiting significant poetry sites courtesy of Red Pine's guidance.

We took a picture in Cold Mountain's cave with that Harrison galley, and I took another picture of water "cold and deep." I included it in a simple picture book I made for each of us opposite of Harrison's poem. It was the trip of a lifetime!

JEFFREY BISHOP, Board Member

Also recommended by **WALTER PARSONS**, Board Member

COLUMBIA UNIV NY ADMIN OFC
2950 BROADWAY 709 JOURNALISM
NEW YORK NY 10027

116018000016 04/04/05
EM14959

TGM1 - TGMA

0509409997323178
MR TED KOOSER CARE JOSEPH BEDNARIK
COPPER CANYON PRESS
FT WORDEN STATE PARK BLDG 313
PORT TOWNSEND WA 98368

4/4/05

YOU WERE AWARDED PULITZER POETRY PRIZE TODAY.

CONGRATULATIONS!

    LEE C BOLLINGER, PRESIDENT
     COLUMBIA UNIVERSITY

MGMCOMP 15:11 EST

On "A Happy Birthday" by Ted Kooser

Interning for Copper Canyon Press deepened my connection to poetry and the poetry community in ways I wouldn't have experienced anywhere else. I read more that summer than any other. The Press's combination of passion for poetry with publishing savvy gifted me with insights I'll always hold close. My bookshelves are heavy with Copper Canyon books.

I read Ted Kooser's "A Happy Birthday" every year on my birthday, a kind of private rite. Its quietude, its gentleness, its quality of endlessness makes every birthday dusk linger in the best possible way.

WESLEY ROTHMAN, Intern

On "On the Road" by Ted Kooser

I knew practically nothing about contemporary poetry before I came to Copper Canyon Press, and the people and the poets there opened the genre to me with such kindness and eagerness. I had heard that Ted Kooser was one of "the greats," but I didn't know what that meant until I read his poem "On the Road." Maybe twice a week, I think about the image of the small pebble that could contain the secrets of the whole universe being picked up, inspected, then warily placed back underfoot. Within so few lines, it says so very much about knowledge, the world around us, and human nature. That's the thing about poetry—it makes you walk the world more slowly, tread more carefully.

HEATHER BRENNAN, Intern

Tim was the first Copper Canyon poet I met through Craig Carlson, my professor at Evergreen. I owe Craig the deepest gratitude for connecting me with Tim and Port Townsend via an internship with Rusty North, who later did a letterpress chapbook of "December Prayer" to support her video documentation of poets.

MARY JANE KNECHT, Development Director and Managing Editor

December Prayer

Tim McNulty
Pawtracks (1978)

For every winter elk
broken off from the herd
alone, as December snows
begin to fill the basin,
ears bowed to the wind

For every blackbear who wakes
midwinter to the steady
gnaw of hunger,
the fall's scant forage not enough
and two months to the thaw

For every ragged coyote
red-stained track
through the crusted snow
carrion long gone and the mice
all safe in their burrows

For you
brothers for whom these months
are a long and bitter night—
may you find in your going
some door, and through it

Down the tangled game trails
of existence:
a place where all the different paths
may join
where we might

Sit down to this poem
together, our many tongues
one

This stunning poem is as elemental as the love it describes—the indelible imprint made on us by who, what, and where we love. This is a new poem from Jane Miller's most recent collection, which is especially thrilling because I've loved and followed her work for decades; she was among the first living poets whose work I found and was instructed by when I was just beginning to take my own writing seriously. She was one of the poets on Copper Canyon Press's list who made me awed and ecstatic to join it. Full disclosure: after many years of knowing and admiring Jane only through her restless, brilliant work, I now know her and love her as a friend. But that's a fitting blessing too: so often Copper Canyon fosters beautiful connections between people as well as through poems.

LISA OLSTEIN, Poet

The Missing Apricot Tree
Jane Miller
Paper Banners (2023)

Long ago, when we met, and had to

separate, you sent a picture

of you squatting by a river,

bathing, your face half-turned, looking

over your shoulder beyond me

into a monastery, and beyond that,

daughters hanging threadbare laundry.

We were ourselves

so young. I longed for your return,

and in springtime, although the wildflowers

were few, we lived together.

Hundreds of fireflies

accompanied us in dream,

swarming in the birches

out the uncurtained windows.

They alarmed us, and the cries of returning geese

drove us farther under the covers.

We never stopped talking of their beauty,

although the years parted us forever.

In the full moon's light

on an empty bed,

the white geese and firefly glow
dissolve. We vanished as gently
as snowfall on a face.
I forgot to give you a parting gift.
Then silence. Not to be confused with emotion.
Anise rises from the village.
And a missing apricot tree
becomes as massive as the past.
The five white petals of its blossom
survive as I do,
as spring energy
in an aging body.
Another night of a big moon.
I roll in and out of its light, wondering,
late autumn, how is it
that I could lose my first love
as carelessly as a line of verse
that made the whole work.
Not that art perishes.
Nor is love
only about pleasure.
I still need to thank
the old gods in the rocky earth
for all that has happened.
This stick will have to be a tree.

One of the early Copper Canyon Press titles—and of course Rexroth was Sam Hamill's guru and a guiding light in the founding of the Press.

ELIOT WEINBERGER, Translator

from "The Silver Swan"

Kenneth Rexroth
The Silver Swan: Poems Written in Kyoto, 1974–75 (1976)

VI

Asagumori

On the forest path
The leaves fall. In the withered
Grass the crickets sing
Their last songs. Through dew and dusk
I walk the paths you once walked,
My sleeves wet with memory.

On "Monopoly" by Connie Wanek

I did not come upon this poem myself. In fact, during the summer of 2011, when I was interning for Copper Canyon—thousands of miles from home in the Deep South—I sent Connie Wanek's collection *On Speaking Terms* to my mother, as I felt she might connect to Wanek's poetry. A week later, my mother called me and said, "Oh my god—have you read the poem 'Monopoly'?" I hadn't. I had been reading Matthew Zapruder and Dean Young. I had barely answered, "No," before she started reading the poem aloud to me over the phone, just as she'd read so many poems to me growing up. And I quickly connected to it just as my mom had, washed away in the poem's images of Monopoly money and the tokens that circle the board in place of our own bodies. Then the turn toward home at the end, the moment when everything that came before in the poem is illuminated in an effortless moment of gusto.

When she finished reading, I had seen every line in the poem in my mind's eye. I had felt its sentiments in my core. There seemed to be so little that my mom and I agreed on anymore, but we were both in awe of this poem and were eager to talk about it. To me, this effect seems to be representative of the Copper Canyon oeuvre: poems that stick to our skin after we read them, that speak across generations, connecting us back to our past and to what we hold most dear.

CHRISTIE COLLINS, Editorial Assistant and Intern

On "The Nurse" by Dana Levin

Dana Levin's "The Nurse" astonished me when I first read it and was the reason, years ago, I wrote Dana Levin a fan letter. (So it was also the poem that led to our long-term friendship.) Levin's vision as a poet has always been cinematic and exciting, and this is no exception.

KEVIN PRUFER, Poet

On "In a Word, a World" by C.D. Wright

The partnership between Copper Canyon Press and C.D. Wright led to some of the most inventive, field-changing, moving, and thoroughly exciting books I've ever read! They enlarged my sense of what poetry could do. They gave me permission.

DANA LEVIN, Poet and APR/ Honickman First Book Prize winner

C.D. Wright was one of the first Copper Canyon poets I encountered, and it is an honor of my lucky life that I was able to learn directly from her while I was a university student. The last three lines of "Lake Echo, Dear" have been ringing in my ears for years, since the first time I read the poem. That final stanza feels like it could be a statement on poetry itself.

NATASHA RAO, APR/Honickman First
Book Prize winner

Lake Echo, Dear

C.D. Wright
Steal Away: Selected and New Poems (2002)

Is the woman in the pool of light
really reading or just staring
at what is written

Is the man walking in the soft rain
naked or is it the rain
that makes his shirt transparent

The boy in the iron cot
is he asleep or still
fingering the springs underneath

Did you honestly believe
three lives could be complete

The bottle of green liquid
on the sill is it real

The bottle on the peeling sill
is it filled with green

Or is the liquid an illusion
of fullness

How summer's children turn
into fish and rain softens men

How the elements of summer
nights bid us to get down with each other
on the unplaned floor

And this feels painfully beautiful
whether or not
it will change the world one drop

This is one of the most recent poems I've loved from a Copper Canyon Press poet—a sign that my long, appreciative relationship with the Press remains current.

WALTER PARSONS, Board Member

Poem Written in a Cab

Alex Dimitrov
Love and Other Poems (2021)

To the people
reading this poem, hello.
I want you to know
nothing bad will happen
as long as you're here.
Every line you see
was written in a cab.
I'm on the FDR
in the middle of winter
and the sky is suddenly bluer
than Sundays in June.
There's no reason for it.
No real science
to what will happen when
I get off at Chambers
and Broadway, wearing
gold and black sneakers
on my way to meet
a friend who is sad.
To my sad friends, hello.
For you I will be
a version of myself
I hardly remember.
I will be a lake
at the top of morning
some late afternoon into night.
And if you look away from
this page, to your right
there's the world.
I am only trying to describe it.
I will likely disappoint you
like a long-awaited date
or like last call at a bar.
The people on Water Street
are leaving work now.

Walking to shops
and to restaurants
or of course to the water—
Manhattan, you are
my favorite island by far.
And I wouldn't be a poet
if I didn't tell you
about the bridges,
there are over two thousand here—
Brooklyn, Verrazzano,
George Washington—
partial hyperbole, partial admission:
I live here for the bridges at night.
It's been so long
since I've taken a vacation
and some days I think,
how is that even possible,
how is this even my life?
I thought I'd be happier
and more handsome,
certainly better loved
and more stable
this late in the day.
But the secret with me
(as I'm sure with you too)
is that everyone thinks
I am fine. Doing great!
What's the point
of saying otherwise
really. It's so gauche
and betrays a self-pity
that probably means
you aren't getting laid.
The mood in Union Square
reminds me of a feeling
I once felt in 1995.
The park looks perfect
and deceptively true.
A gorgeous blond
is smoking a joint
and reading, not
waiting for anyone
and refusing to look up.
Maybe he will
but it just doesn't

seem like today
is the day to get
his attention.
He's already turning
the page and so focused,
whatever he's reading
it's all that he is.
And just so you know
we're in a different cab now,
in another month
with better weather—
goodbye to the past!
It's important
to look at something
you can't have
at least once a day.
Like the blond
a few lines up.
Perhaps you should
even touch it
or put it in your mouth.
When people kiss in public
it's a sign you're not alone.
Even if you're not the one
being kissed, there's something
obviously human about it.
And to be obvious is boring
except for real sentiment
or standing naked
in front of someone.
We're all either kissing
or pissing on each other.
Everything in between
is too safe to comment on
and not poetry in the least.
Once I was 19
and now I'm 33.
I used to prefer autumn
but spring has made me an adult.
The silence on Charles Street
is charming, even though it's
nothing like the silence I know,
which can't be compared to
a street or anything modern
despite this being

a New York poem.
Still, I'm going to try
because what else is there to do
other than work
and down gin and tonics.
There's a minute
right before the cab
drops me off
when I think—*don't stop,
take me anywhere else.
Just keep driving!
I have it all wrong.*
I have it all wrong
but I'm somehow alive.
Some things never change
and why would you want them to.
Like Katz's deli,
where I still haven't eaten
but take comfort
in knowing it's there.
Or the Flatiron building
where I've been once or twice,
and where my friend
Dorothea and I took photos
in an elevator and talked about
why it's important
to keep going no matter what.
Poets are doing this constantly
and it's one way of showing people
possibility is real and invented.
It has to come from the self!
It doesn't just show up one day.
You have to leave your house
to make eyes with someone
over a kale salad. Sometimes
you have to dye your hair blond
to remember you're truly a brunette.
Whenever I see people
crying on First Avenue
I think of the times
I've cried on First Avenue—
which is, by all standards,
a great avenue to cry on.
Like Janis Joplin's
"Get It While You Can"

is a great song and one
that's extended my life
on many occasions.
Not scientifically
but undeniably spiritually.
And stay with me now
as this is the part of the poem
where I'm trying to tell you
life is better than death
and more ridiculous too.
This is hard to know
given the day or the season,
but I have to trust myself
since I'm likely
the most neurotic poet
in the room, and maybe someone
you'll know in another life
when we come back as dogs.
The thing is, the world
will continue without us
just as this poem will continue
even if there's no one
to read what it says.
Please keep reading.
I care so much that you do.
I want to be in rooms
and cabs together,
listening to everything
that's ever happened to us
until some point in the story
when all the details
are out of the way
and there's nothing left to say
except the simplest things.
I don't know what they are
but on Bleecker Street
at half past noon on a Wednesday
two boys are pointing
at a billboard
or studying the sky.
Whatever they're thinking of,
it's not about the end of the world.
One of them is wearing
an orange hat and the other
has a button on his backpack

that says "M E O W."
Exactly! Only yesterday
I spoke to everyone like a cat.
Which is to say, I was mysterious
and pleasing to myself.
I stopped confusing
my body for a weapon
but my body has never
impressed me.
I'm Slavic, after all.
I don't believe in
self-love, which is
a kind of American sadness
that often feels
desperate and dull.
It's powerful to feel
you can change
even small things,
even things that don't
seem to matter at all.
Like the arch of your eyebrows
or the color of your lips
(both of which,
now that I think of it,
are very important and real).
Like being at a party
and for less than a second
feeling like someone entirely new.
I have never wanted to be myself.
What a ludicrous obligation!
Having a fantasy
is the least sad thing there is
and the only thing
that gets me out of bed.
Which makes me think
I should sit down
and write a list
of my fantasies
or at least the things
I love about the world.
Maybe the list will be so long
I'll call it "Love"
and turn it into a book,
allowing me to feel
justified in not taking more cabs

as a way to finish this poem.
In any case, whenever
I'm in California
I want to be in New York.
And whenever
I'm in New York
I'd rather be in London
because the rain is like light there,
it has this way of calming me down.
It's 9:14 pm
and the cab I'm in now
is on West 8th Street
almost at the Marlton Hotel
where I'm going on a date.
I have no choice but to follow
my idea of romance,
which as it turns out
means checking my hair
on my phone, like a mirror,
and after too many drinks
telling a man that my favorite word
is *bijou*—French for jewel.
Haven't I suffered enough
terrible dates! Couldn't this
be the one that changes
my life and comes with
a house in the Hamptons.
I can never fall asleep
with a stranger in bed
unless it's their own bed
and feels like the aisle seat
on a flight to Europe.
Which is to say—
there's an escape!
Or at least a way
to attend to your needs.
There's a freedom in hotel bars
when telling the bartender a secret
or switching up your drink
can remind you life isn't over.
That maybe it's just stalled for a while.
Usually my drink is champagne
or prosecco. Red wine
with my friend Will,
Diet Coke with Melissa,

and anything anywhere
with my longest friend
Rachel, who everyone knows
wears all black. Marya
does this lovely thing
where she asks for a glass of seltzer
and pours half of it in her rosé.
I really think she's invented
something necessary,
she's a Pisces after all.
And Deborah is classic.
I find her commitment
to cocktails an admirable choice.
I can never remember
which one exactly
because I'm always looking
at her hair, which has never
looked bad in the ten years
I've known her, and that's glamour.
If I had to define glamour
that's what I'd say it is.
Now there's no smooth way
to make this transition
but I'm in another cab again,
weeks later, trying to remember
who that guy from the date even was,
or why I said I'd text but never did,
as it usually happens with me.
I'm very close to taking out a loan
because of these cab rides.
If any patrons or arts organizations
are reading this, feel free
to send me a check or give me a call.
My number is 248 760 3425.
I think one thing
people misunderstand about me
is how ironic I am
in almost every aspect of life.
I can barely put on pants
to smoke a cigarette
but I'm absolutely dedicated
to writing a good sentence.
I wonder what my mother is doing
at exactly this moment.
I wonder if the L train
has ever taken anyone

where they needed to go.
When I was younger
all I wanted was to be taken seriously.
A serious poet! Why not.
Now I realize being taken seriously
is as arbitrary as how long you live.
I would gladly trade wisdom for youth.
Or beauty. Or the way I stood
in the corner at parties,
always complaining how boring
they were, how we should have gone
somewhere else or maybe
shouldn't have gone out at all.
Please go to parties, everyone.
Even if it's just to see
people you dread
drinking very warm beer.
Sometimes there's justice
in the world! And sometimes
you end up being
that dreadful person
drinking warm beer
and hating yourself.
I can't believe my fare is
already 17 dollars.
We're stuck in traffic
on 28th and 2nd
and I'm going to be late
but making it across town
with feeling, no less!
My driver just told me
he's Russian and I said
"oh great, I'm Bulgarian,
where in Russia exactly?"
He found this absurd
because he laughed
and said "Moscow,"
and now he's asking me
when it was that I came to America
and I'm telling him
in this roundabout way
how I was six and how
it was very hard on my parents
because we were poor
and I was the only one
who spoke English.

But I'll leave that
for later. Or never.
I'll leave you with a few
thoughts on the imagination
because the imagination
is a wild thought
and more honest
than biography.
What's happened to us
is unimportant.
Terrible things
happen to people
all the time.
It's about the day
and more than the day.
It's everything between me
and my cab driver from Moscow,
getting me to my meeting
without a hint of panic or luck.
"How long have you
lived here," I ask
and he says thirty years
which is crazy to me.
"Only twelve," I tell him.
But I actually love this so much
because for a second I'm young
in this cab, or at least
someone younger.
There's a loud bang
on Madison and I remember
that tomorrow's my birthday.
Oh god. Once again.
November 30, 1984.
It's been a while
and it's been a lot.
It's been romantic
but I definitely want more.
I have no plans
yet can easily make them.
There's rarely enough money
but surely it's possible
to walk down the street
and have coffee alone.
I put in my headphones
and listen to Nico's
"These Days"

before my meeting.
It's such a good song,
I can't believe that it's real.
So good in fact,
that for however long
I forget about everything.
New York is New York.
My life is decidedly mine.
Then I start worrying I haven't
worn enough sunscreen
and will someday die of
cancer. I start worrying
I won't die of cancer
but be forgotten and old.
I'm so dramatic.
I'm not even a poet.
I'm really an actor.
And almost at 34 now,
yes, I do think
I look great for my age.
I ate an egg and an orange
for breakfast. My beard
is quite long and still
very well groomed.
It's incredible really,
even to me, who rarely
feels accomplished
or takes compliments,
that anyone can make it this far.

Poems for Tomorrow

... come celebrate
with me that everyday
something has tried to kill me
and has failed.
— Lucille Clifton

Somewhere Lucille Clifton said, "I choose
joy because I am capable of it,
and there are others who are not."
I carry this poem in my heart.
Thank you, Lucille Clifton & Copper Canyon.
Ellen Bass

It isn't one line that sticks with me; it's the sheer variety of lines, of forms, of voice, all the wild incarnations of language. It's the differences between all these lines of poetry ringing out of Copper Canyon. It isn't one line, one poem, or one poet. It is, all of it taken together, a portrait of poetry, a half century of living and writing and dying that sticks with me.

— Jeswander boline

On "A House Called Tomorrow" by Alberto Ríos

Alberto Ríos's "A House Called Tomorrow" makes my heart sing. It is a loving reminder that we walk in the words and works of all those who came before us and that our greatest imperative is to move forward in hope. As a writer, I am called by this poem to create; as a human being, I am called to honor the past and to be of service to the future.

JULIE CHRISTINE JOHNSON, Finance and Operations Manager

On "Suppressing the Evidence" by Carolyn Kizer

Carolyn Kizer asks us: "How may we bear witness, as we should?"

With protest, elegy, clarity, voice, vision, craft. Looking straight on at our own failings. Saying it anyway.

KRIS BECKER, Development Manager and Office Manager

On "Indispensable" by James Richardson

I read James Richardson's "Indispensable" for the first time when I was an intern at Copper Canyon Press. It was early morning, the sunlight was streaming across the page, and I heard the birds singing outside my window in Port Townsend. This poem struck me at just the right moment—it spoke to the interconnectedness of the human world, the natural world, and how even the smallest actions have repercussions beyond our immediate notice.

As the effects of global climate change have accelerated over the past half decade since this poem was published, as we grapple with war, political polarization, a pandemic, and disasters both man-made and natural, I've turned to these words again and again as a kind of aphorism—a reminder that everything is connected.

RON MARTIN-DENT, Intern

I return to Bob Hicok's *Elegy Owed* a lot. There's a conversational tone to these elegies that lures you in, but the elegies are also surrealist aerograms bringing messages from the future, moving us in unexpected ways. This poem, for me, sums up the absurdity of the human condition in the most heartbreaking, perfect way.

TISHANI DOSHI, Poet

Ode to ongoing

Bob Hicok
Elegy Owed (2013)

People are having babies. Hoisting their children
to tree limbs on their backs and tying their shoes.
Telling them what the numerator is and why not
to eat one's boogers or not publicly
pee if at all possible to pee in private.
People are mixing their genes after wine
in romantic alleys and London hotels after crossing
a famous bridge. Trying to save for college
and not hit their children like they were hit
and not hit their children differently
than they were hit and failing and succeeding.
People are singing to wombs and playing the Goldberg
variations to fetuses who'll love Glenn Gould
without knowing who Glenn Gould is. I'm driving
along or painting a board or wondering
if we love animals because we can't talk with them
more intimately than we can't talk with God
and the whole time there's this background hum
of sex and devotion and fear, people telling
good-night stories or leaving their babies
in dumpsters but mostly working hard
to feed the future what it needs to grow strong
and prefer sweet over sour, consonance
to dissonance, to be the only creatures who notice
the stars or at least use them metaphorically
to go on and on about the longing we harbor
in such tiny spaces relative to the extent
of our dread that we're in this alone.

All were touched by Swir's poems, moved by their depth and insight, their potent coupling of humor and darkness—as if, in the end, she might bring the body and the soul together again.

DAVID ROMTVEDT, Poet

The Soul and the Body on the Beach

Anna Swir, translated from the Polish
by Czesław Miłosz and Leonard Nathan
Talking to My Body (1996)

The soul on the beach
studies a textbook of philosophy.
The soul asks the body:
Who bound us together?
The body says:
Time to tan the knees.

The soul asks the body:
Is it true
that we do not really exist?
The body says:
I'm tanning my knees.

The soul asks the body:
Where will the dying begin,
in you or in me?
The body laughs.
It tanned its knees.

This is my favorite poem from *Solar Perplexus*. I love the imagery and tone of hopefulness the poem dances around. I often think of the lines "The kaleidoscope remains the most / efficacious diagnostic instrument / for those of us who've been shattered."

LILY SADIGHMEHR, Intern

Silly String

Dean Young
Solar Perplexus (2019)

A seat is being prepared for us
in the rain.
A lily has been prepared.
The catalogue of loss comes to an end
regardless of the punctuation.
If you stopped reading at page 45,
Gatsby never dies,
the rules that govern this whole operatic shtick
written down and erased so many times,
who's surprised a marriage turns into
mush, a vow just idiot sound?
Pretty much doesn't mean a thing
like most hymns.
And for those of us looking ahead,
there interposes an ambulance.
Someone's washing chrysanthemums
in the parking lot. Someone's hefting
body-size bags of dog food into a truck.
The kaleidoscope remains the most
efficacious diagnostic instrument
for those of us who've been shattered.
There's so much I can't explain
if someone would just give me the chance.

On "the silence will be sudden then last" by Deborah Landau

I heard Landau read from this work in Brooklyn in 2019. I remember being deeply affected, shaken even, by the urgency of her reading. It emerged in the heart of the Trump terror and targeting. A dark cloud hovered ominously and everywhere in the atmosphere of the time. Landau's work speaks to the menace and vulnerability that so palpably continues to define much of our current condition. The feminine, especially, is powerfully sketched out in the face of bracing aggression that continues to define the era. The title *Soft Targets* . . . so apt.

JEFFREY BISHOP, Board Member

On "On a Portrait of Two Beauties" by Hồ Xuân Hương, translated from the Nôm by John Balaban

Hồ Xuân Hương, an eighteenth-century CE Vietnamese poet, offers us entry into the life and times of a woman who transcended many of the constraints of her background and her society. For her to write at all was a triumph. Not only do I love the limpid quality of her observations, but I'm also grateful to John Balaban, her translator, for his work in keeping a uniquely Vietnamese voice present for us. Hồ Xuân Hương's work was written in Nôm, a writing system that represented Vietnamese speech rather than Mandarin, which was the language of the day's elites. As a speaker of Basque, I am drawn to this support for minority languages.

DAVID ROMTVEDT, Poet

On "Prayer" by Amanda Gunn

Sometimes you find a poem that makes you say, "I wish I wrote that." "Prayer" from Amanda Gunn's debut, *Things I Didn't Do with This Body,* is one of these poems. Within her gorgeous tribute to her own body, I find a testament to women's bodies everywhere: their forms, their beauty, their capacity for strength. It reminds me of what my body has done, what it can do, but most of all, it reminds me to be gentle with myself.

KACI X. TAVARES, Development Manager, Publishing Fellow, and Intern

On "Recurring Dreams" by Monica Sok

I am in awe of how Sok expresses her story of the Cambodian diaspora, as well as her take on racism, America, and family. "Recurring Dreams" gives a glimpse of dreams and reality blended into one, her interaction with family, and reclamation of culture and self through the line *"You must know. Your history."*

ASELA LEE KEMPER, Intern

On "won't you celebrate with me" by Lucille Clifton

At this moment in its history, Copper Canyon Press seeks to expand its commitment to diversity, equity, and inclusion in all aspects. In Lucille's poem "won't you celebrate with me," she writes about poetic creation and self-definition as "both nonwhite and woman." She declares that she has "no model," yet she serves as the ultimate model for all poets on the diversity spectrum because of the courage and audacity of her vision. She was also unflappable in most situations, as Michael can attest!

ROZ ANDERSON FLOOD, Board Member

That ending! "You can trust me, / there is no planet stranger / than the one i'm from." The speaker's kinship with Superman—a literal alien in America—speaks to something fundamental about what it means to live in and observe this country, this planet, as an outsider. Superheroes hold a lot of mythological weight in American culture, and seeing Clifton wield that weight in her deft poems—wow. She's a legend for a reason.

KATE O'DONOGHUE, Intern

note, passed to superman

Lucille Clifton
The Book of Light (1993)

sweet jesus, superman,
if i had seen you
dressed in your blue suit
i would have known you.
maybe that choirboy clark
can stand around
listening to stories
but not you, not with
metropolis to save
and every crook in town
filthy with kryptonite.
lord, man of steel,
i understand the cape,
the leggings, the whole
ball of wax.
you can trust me,
there is no planet stranger
than the one i'm from.

I was in graduate school trying to translate Georg Trakl and Rainer Maria Rilke. I had been working on a translation of Rilke's "Leda" without success and decided to go to the local bookstore, where I found a copy of Lucille Clifton's *The Book of Light*. I can't tell you why I picked it up, but I did and opened it, rather randomly, to her astonishing series of poems "leda 1," "leda 2," and "leda 3." I remember being frozen there in the store.

Translation is also an act of interpretation, but what Clifton does with the Leda myth, gender, power reversal, language, and voice is mesmerizing. They are persona poems, spoken in the increasingly personal and angry voice of Leda, but without the distance one normally feels from a persona poem. These are vital, urgent, present, immediate poems. The past is present; the present is on fire, and fire can't burn like these lyrics.

For centuries, men have made lush paintings, sculpture, and poetry about Leda's rape, but this was the first time I had read the myth through the lens of a woman's experience of sexual assault. "There is nothing luminous," the poem begins. These poems function as a form of justice—justice for Leda, justice for Clifton, justice for all survivors.

DEAN RADER, Poet

leda [1, 2, 3]
Lucille Clifton
The Book of Light (1993)

leda 1

there is nothing luminous
about this.
they took my children.
i live alone in the backside
of the village.
my mother moved
to another town. my father
follows me around the well,
his thick lips slavering,
and at night my dreams are full
of the cursing of me
fucking god fucking me.

leda 2

sometimes another star chooses.
the ones coming in from the east
are dagger-fingered men,
princes of no known kingdom.
the animals are raised up in their stalls
battering the stable door.
sometimes it all goes badly;
the inn is strewn with feathers,
the old husband suspicious,
and the fur between her thighs
is the only shining thing.

leda 3

a personal note (re: visitations)

always pyrotechnics;
stars spinning into phalluses
of light, serpents promising
sweetness, their forked tongues
thick and erect, patriarchs of bird
exposing themselves in the air.
this skin is sick with loneliness.
You want what a man wants,
next time come as a man
or don't come.

Yes, yes, I am working on self-love, body positivity, accepting my ever-softening body and sagging breasts. And I genuinely love my gray hair and the hard-won knowledge of who I am. But aging is a ride. Olena Kalytiak Davis captures the ambivalence surrounding this process with the wryness, humor, dread, and nuance we deserve. This poem is, as the kids say, #middleagegoals.

ANGELA GARBES, Publicist and Intern

Decline

Olena Kalytiak Davis
Late Summer Ode (2022)

Both down and no. The mal de mer
of facing what's clearcut:
these un-fine lines, the well-defined
slack and brace of time time time.

Glimpsed this etching first
in the summer of nineteen
ninety six: not possible; can no longer
fool: it's worn, it's ripped. Youth took this ship.

Youth hung on every fucking sail. Once,
sought south, sought light, sought
so low, to quicken and to slow.
Went too fast. Went too slow, some low flame

of having been. So many spots of sun, of sex,
and yet wasn't, didn't exist
on none of those days. Now
fading and waving: no, no, no.

Goes on too long. Too short. Over spent
and over wrought. So many and you want
them back? Such plain panic, such much
suffering stilled and still it returns—
but it is over over over.

Had my days and can not name them.
In the new nausea of nostalgia: will
have come to this. this. this.
this exact: moment of *is*.

When I was introduced to Copper Canyon Press, I began to learn about the poetry of Natalie Diaz, who had a fellowship at Princeton at the time. Natalie's "The Last Mojave Indian Barbie" is a brilliant parody of the use of a popular doll to impose cultural norms on America's girls. In it, Natalie skillfully uses humor and pathos to imagine a Barbie reborn on the "rez." She powerfully skewers both dominant white cultural representation and commercialization; as such, her poetry makes the case for prominent inclusion of Indigenous poets among Copper Canyon Press titles.

ROZ ANDERSON FLOOD, Board Member

The Last Mojave Indian Barbie

Natalie Diaz
When My Brother Was an Aztec (2012)

Wired to her display box were a pair of one-size-fits-all-Indians stiletto moccasins, faux turquoise earrings, a dream catcher, a copy of *Indian Country Today*, erasable markers for chin and forehead tattoos, and two six-packs of mini magic beer bottles—when tilted up, the bottles turned clear, when turned right-side-up, the bottles refilled. Mojave Barbie repeatedly drank Ken and Skipper under their pink plastic patio table sets. Skipper said she drank like a boy.

Mojave Barbie secretly hated the color of her new friends' apricot skins, how they burned after riding in Ken's convertible Camaro with the top down, hated how their micro hairbrushes tangled and knotted in her own thick, black hair, which they always wanted to braid. There wasn't any diet cola in their cute little ice chests, and worst of all, Mojave Barbie couldn't find a single soft spot on her body to inject her insulin. It had taken years of court cases, litigation, letters from tribal council members, testimonials from CHR nurses, and a few diabetic comas just to receive permission to buy the never-released hypodermic needle accessory kit—before that, she'd bought most on the Japanese black market—Mattel didn't like toying around with the possibility of a Junkie Barbie.

Mojave Barbie had been banned from the horse stables and was no longer invited to dinner, not since she let it slip that when the cavalry came to Fort Mojave, the Mojaves ate a few horses. It had happened, and she only let it slip after Skipper tried to force her to admit the Mojave Creation was just a myth: *It's true. I'm from Spirit Mountain,* Mojave Barbie had said. *No, you're not,* Skipper had argued. *You came from Asia.* But Mojave Barbie wasn't missing much—they didn't have lazy man's bread or tortillas in the Barbie Stovetop to Tabletop Deluxe Kitchen. In fact, they only had a breakfast set, so they ate the same two sunny-side-up eggs and pancakes every meal.

Each night after dinner, Mojave Barbie sneaked from the guesthouse—next to the tennis courts and Hairtastic Salon—to rendezvous with Ken, sometimes in the collapsible Glamour Camper, but most often in the Dream Pool. She would *yenni* Ken all night long. (*Yenni* was the Mojave word for sex, explained a culturally informative booklet included in Mojave Barbie's box, along with an authentic frybread recipe, her Certificate of Indian Blood, a casino player's card, and a voided per capita check.) They took precautions to prevent waking others inside the Dream House—Mojave Barbie's tan webbed hand covering Ken's always-open mouth muffled his ejaculations.

One night, after drinking a pint of Black Velvet disguised as a bottle of suntan lotion, Ken felt especially playful. Ken was wild, wanted to sport his plastic Stetson and pleather holsters, wanted Mojave Barbie to wear her traditional outfit, still twist-tied to her box. She agreed and donned her mesquite-bark skirt and went shirtless except for strands of blue and white glass beads that hung down in coils around her neck. The single feather in her hair tickled Ken's fancy. He begged Mojave Barbie to wrap her wide, dark hips around him in the "Mojave Death Grip," an indigenous love maneuver that made him thankful for his double-jointed pelvis. (A Mojave Death Grip Graphic How-To Manual was once included in the culturally informative booklet, but a string of disjointed legs and a campaign by the Girl Scouts of America led to a recall.) Ken pointed his wooden six-shooter and chased her up the Dream Slide. The weight of the perfectly proportioned bodies sent the pool accessory crashing to the patio. Every light in every window painted itself on as the Dream House swung open from the middle, giving all inside a sneak peek at naked Ken's hard body and naked Mojave Barbie gripping his pistol, both mid-yenni and dripping wet.

Ken was punished by Mattel's higher-ups, had his tennis racket, tuxedo, Limited Edition Hummer, scuba and snorkel gear, aviator sunglasses, Harley, windjammer sailboard, his iPad and iPhone confiscated. Mojave Barbie had been caught red-handed and bare-breasted. She was being relocated—a job dealing blackjack at some California casino. On her way out the gate, she kicked the plastic cocker spaniel, which fell sideways but never pulled its tongue in or even barked—she felt an ache behind her 39 EE left breast for her rez dog, which had been discontinued long ago. Mojave Barbie tossed a trash bag filled with clothes and accessories into her primered Barbie Happy Family Volvo, which she'd bought at a yard sale. The car had hidden beneath a tarp in the Dream House driveway since she got there. She climbed through the passenger door over to the driver's seat, an explosion of ripped vinyl, towels, and duct tape. She pumped and pumped the gas pedal, clicked and clicked the ignition, until the jalopy fired up. Mojave Barbie rolled away, her mismatched hubcaps wobbling and rattling, a book of yellow WIC coupons rustling on the dash, and a Joy Harjo tape melted in the tape deck blaring, *I'm not afraid to be hungry. I'm not afraid to be full.*

Mom and Dad Barbie, Grandma Barbie, Skipper, and Ken stood on the Dream House balcony and watched Mojave Barbie go. Grandma Barbie tilted at the waist whispering to Mom Barbie, *They should've kept that one in the cupboard.* Dad Barbie piped in, *Yep, it's always a gamble with those people.* Mom Barbie was silent, hoping the purpling, bruise-like marks the size of mouths circling Ken's neck were not what she thought they were: hickies, or, as the culturally informative booklet explained, a "Mojave necklace." Skipper complained to Ken that Mojave Barbie had flipped them off as she drove out the wrought-iron gates, which, of course, locked behind her with a clang. Ken fingered the blue bead in his pocket and reassured Skipper, *Mojave Barbie was probably waving goodbye—with hands like that, you can never be sure.*

This poem crushes me. It cuts, quivers, and calls out a legacy of American conquest over the Indigenous body. Easily one of the most unforgettable poems I have ever read.

MICHAEL WASSON, Poet

Also recommended by NICHOLAS SEOW, Intern

Abecedarian Requiring Further Examination of Anglikan Seraphym Subjugation of a Wild Indian Rezervation

Natalie Diaz
When My Brother Was an Aztec (2012)

Angels don't come to the reservation.
Bats, maybe, or owls, boxy mottled things.
Coyotes, too. They all mean the same thing—
death. And death
eats angels, I guess, because I haven't seen an angel
fly through this valley ever.
Gabriel? Never heard of him. Know a guy named Gabe though—
he came through here one powwow and stayed, typical
Indian. Sure he had wings,
jailbird that he was. He flies around in stolen cars. Wherever he stops,
kids grow like gourds from women's bellies.
Like I said, no Indian I've ever heard of has ever been or seen an angel.
Maybe in a Christmas pageant or something—
Nazarene church holds one every December,
organized by Pastor John's wife. It's no wonder
Pastor John's son is the angel—everyone knows angels are white.
Quit bothering with angels, I say. They're no good for Indians.
Remember what happened last time
some white god came floating across the ocean?
Truth is, there may be angels, but if there are angels
up there, living on clouds or sitting on thrones across the sea wearing
velvet robes and golden rings, drinking whiskey from silver cups,
we're better off if they stay rich and fat and ugly and
'xactly where they are—in their own distant heavens.
You better hope you never see angels on the rez. If you do, they'll be
        marching you off to
Zion or Oklahoma, or some other hell they've mapped out for us.

This poem makes me cry, hurt, ache—Aimee, who is known for her joy, shows us her power and skill in writing about the atrocity that is child sex slavery. Not an easy read, but an important one.

KELLI RUSSELL AGODON, Poet

Two Moths

Aimee Nezhukumatathil
Oceanic (2018)

Some girls   on the other side of this planet

will never know   the loveliness

of walking   in a crepe silk sari.   Instead

they will spend   their days   on their backs

for a parade of men   who could be   their uncles

in another life.   These girls memorize

each slight wobble   of fan blade as it cuts

through the stale   tea air and auto-rickshaw

exhaust   thick as egg curry.

Men   shove greasy rupees   at the door

for one hour   in a room

with a twelve-year-old.   One hour—   One hour—

One hour.   And if she cries afterward

her older sister   will cover it up.   Will rim

the waterline   of her eyes   with kohl pencil

until it looks like   two popinjay moths

have stopped   to rest   on her exquisite   face.

Seeing the patriarchy for what it is. Unabashed feminism. These are learned skills for me. Skills that I learned, in large part, through poems like Perillo's "Dangerous Life." This is a poem I return to for its blunt honesty, humor, and, more than anything, the way it compels me to be exactly the woman I want to be.

SIERRA GOLDEN, Intern

Dangerous Life
Lucia Perillo
Time Will Clean the Carcass Bones: Selected and New Poems (2016)

I quit med school when I found out the stiff they gave me
had book 9 of *Paradise Lost* and the lyrics
to "Louie Louie" tattooed on her thighs.

That morning as the wind was mowing
little ladies on a street below, I touched a Bunsen burner
to the Girl Scout sash whose badges were the measure of my worth:

Careers ...
Cookery, Seamstress ...
and *Baby Maker* ... all gone up in smoke.

But I kept the merit badge marked *Dangerous Life,*
for which, if you remember, the girls were taken to the woods
and taught the mechanics of fire,

around which they had us dance with pointed sticks
lashed into crucifixes that we'd wrapped with yarn and wore
on lanyards round our necks, calling them our "Eyes of God."

Now my mother calls the pay phone outside my walk-up, raving
about what people think of a woman—thirty, unsettled,
living on food stamps, coin-op Laundromats & public clinics.

Some nights I take my lanyards from their shoebox, practice baying
those old camp songs to the moon. And remember how they told us
that a smart girl could find her way out of anywhere, alive.

On "The East-West Border" by Jaan Kaplinski, translated from the Estonian by the author with Sam Hamill and Riina Tamm

"The East-West Border" by Kaplinski says it all—the politics of countries, of shifting borders, and those of the heart. *The Wandering Border* is also the first of several Copper Canyon Press books to feature Pacific Northwest artist George Tsutakawa on the cover.

MARY JANE KNECHT, Development Director and Managing Editor

On "Having our cake and being eaten by it, too" by Bob Hicok

I like the directness, clarity, and specificity of Hicok's poems, particularly in his poem "Having our cake and being eaten by it, too." For me, poetry is at its best when the words and language connect to the very center of me. Being in community with others who experience the same thing is my favorite part of being a Copper Canyon board member.

DONNA BELLEW, Board Member

On *Still Another Day* by Pablo Neruda, translated from the Spanish by William O'Daly

The diaphanous mystery of a question well-worded in poetic terms is in full bloom in this Nerudian poem. *Still Another Day* is a masterpiece of modern poetry by a prodigious wordsmith.

DAVID HUERTA, Poet

On "Contact" by Camille Rankine

"Contact" is an enduring poem; I find meaning, or beauty, or clarity in a new line upon every reading. Right now, it feels especially poignant. After nearly two years of little to no contact with others and social distancing, Camille Rankine's words land differently: "Today, a near collision / with a stranger. How I tried to touch, be / known. To think a body moves me, moves / for me. To think it doesn't."

Rankine has a way of writing about grief that holds the reader. My family lost our grandfather to COVID-19 last year, and I can't help but think of this loss in one of her final lines in the poem: "How we bury our living / within us." How beautiful it is to be reminded of that.

JACKIE DELANEY, Intern

Water Calligraphy

Arthur Sze
Sight Lines (2019)

I

A green turtle in broth is brought to the table—
I stare at an irregular formation of rocks

above a pond and spot, on the water's
surface, a moon. As I step back and forth,

the moon slides from partial to full
to partial and then into emptiness; but no

moon's in the sky, just slanting sunlight,
leafing willows along Slender West Lake,

parked cars outside an apartment complex
where, against a background of chirping birds

and car horns, two women bicker. Now
it's midnight at noon; I hear an electric saw

and the occasional sound of lumber striking
pavement. At the bottom of a teacup,

leaves form the character *individual*
and, after a sip, the number *eight*.

Snipped into pieces, a green turtle is returned
to the table; while everyone eats,

strands of thrown silk tighten, tighten
in my gut. I blink, and a woodblock carver

peels off pear shavings, stroke by stroke,
and foregrounds characters against empty space.

Begging in a subway, a blind teen and his mother stagger through the swaying car—

a woman lights a bundle of incense and bows at a cauldron—

people raise their palms around the Nine-Dragon Juniper—

who knows the mind of a watermelon vendor picking his teeth?—

you glance up through layers of walnut leaves in a courtyard—

biting into marinated lotus stems—

in a drum tower, hours were measured
as water rising then spilling from one kettle into another—

pomegranate trees flowering along a highway—

climbing to the top of a pagoda, you look down at rebuilt city walls—

a peacock cries—

always the clatter of mah-jongg tiles behind a door—

at a tower loom, a man and woman weave brocade silk—

squashing a cigarette above a urinal, a bus driver hurries back—

a musician strikes sticks, faster and faster—

cars honk along a street approaching a traffic circle—

when he lowers his fan, the actor's face has changed from black to white—

a child squats and shits in a palace courtyard—

yellow construction cranes pivot over the tops of high-rise apartments—

a woman throws a shuttle with green silk through the shed—

where are we headed, you wonder, as you pick a lychee and start to peel it—

3

Lightning ignites a fire in the wilderness: in hours,
200 then 2,000 acres are aflame; when a hotshot
crew hikes in to clear lines, a windstorm
kicks up and veers the blaze back, traps them,
and their fire shelters become their body bags.
Piñons in the hills have red and yellow needles—
in a bamboo park, a woman dribbles liquefied sugar
onto a plate, and it cools, on a stick, in the form
of a butterfly; a man in red pants stills
then moves through the Crane position.
A droplet hangs at the tip of a fern—water
spills into another kettle; you visualize
how flames engulfed them at 50 miles per hour.
In the West, wildfires scar each summer—
water beads on beer cans at a lunch counter—
you do not want to see exploding propane tanks;
you try to root in the world, but events sizzle
along razor wire, along a snapping end of a power line.

4

Two fawns graze on leaves in a yard—
as we go up the Pearl Tower, I gaze
through smog at freighters along the river.
A thunderstorm gathers: it rains and hails
on two hikers in the Barrancas; the arroyo
becomes a torrent, and they crouch for an hour.
After a pelting storm, you spark into flame
and draw the wax of the world into light—
ostrich and emu eggs in a basket by the door,
the aroma of cumin and pepper in the air.
In my mouth, a blister forms then disappears.
At a teak table, with family and friends,
we eat Dungeness crab, but, as I break
apart shell and claws, I hear a wounded elk
shot in the bosque. Canoers ask and receive
permission to land; they beach a canoe
with a yellow cedar wreath on the bow
then catch a bus to the fairgrounds powwow.

5

—Sunrise: I fill my rubber bucket with water
　　　and come to this patch of blue-gray sidewalk—
I've made a sponge-tipped brush at the end
　　　of a waist-high plastic stick; and, as I dip it,
I know water is my ink, memory my blood—

the tips of purple bamboo arch over the park—
　　　I see a pitched battle at the entrance to a palace
and rooftops issuing smoke and flames—
　　　today, there's a white statue of a human figure,
buses and cars drive across the blank square—

at that time, I researched carp in captivity
　　　and how they might reproduce and feed
people in communes—I might have made
　　　a breakthrough, but Red Guards knocked at the door—
they beat me, woke me up at all hours

until I didn't know whether it was midnight or noon—
　　　I saw slaughtered pigs piled on wooden racks,
snow in the spring sunshine—the confessions
　　　they handed me I signed—I just wanted it
to end—then herded pigs on a farm—wait—

a masseur is striking someone's back,
　　　his hands clatter like wooden blocks—
now I block the past by writing the present—
　　　as I write the strokes of *moon*, I let the brush
~~swerve~~ rest for a moment before I lift it

and make the one ~~stroke~~ hook—ah, it's all
　　　in that hook—there, I levitate: no mistakes
will last, even regret is lovely—my hand
　　　trembles; but if I find the ~~gaps~~ resting places,
I cut the sinews of an ox, even as the ~~sun~~

moon waxes—the bones drop, my brush is sharp,
　　　sharper than steel—and though people murmur
at the evaporating characters, I smile, ~~frown~~
　　　fidget, let go—I draw the white, not the black—

6

Tea leaves in the cup spell *above* then *below*—
outside the kitchen window, a spray

of wisteria blossoms in May sunshine.
What unfolds inside us? We sit at a tabletop

that was once a wheel in Thailand: an iron hoop
runs along the rim. On a fireplace mantel,

a flame flickers at the bottom of a metal cup.
As spokes to a hub, a chef cleans blowfish:

turtles beach on white sand: a monk rakes
gravel into scalloped waves in a garden:

moans issue from an alley where men stir
from last night's binge. If all time converges

as light from stars, all situations reside here.
In red-edged heat, I irrigate the peach trees;

you bake a zucchini frittata; water buffalo
browse in a field; hail has shredded lettuces,

and, as a farmer paces and surveys damage,
a coyote slips across a road, under barbed wire.

7

The letter A was once an inverted cow's head,
but now, as I write, it resembles feet
planted on the earth rising to a point.

Once is glimpsing the Perseid meteor shower—
and, as emotion curves space, I find
a constellation that arcs beyond the visible.

A neighbor brings cucumbers and basil;
when you open the bag and inhale, the world
inside is fire in a night courtyard

at summer solstice; we have limned the time here
and will miss the bamboo arcing along
the fence behind our bedroom, peonies

leaning to earth. A *mayordomo* retrenches
the opening to the ditch; water runs near
the top of juniper poles that line our length—

in the bosque, the elk carcass decomposes
into a stench of antlers and bones. Soon
ducks will nest on the pond island, and as

a retired violinist who fed skunks left a legacy—
one she least expected—we fold this
in our pocket and carry it wherever we go.

On "Let Me Try Again" by Javier Zamora

Javier Zamora's poetry, based upon his experience as a nine-year-old unaccompanied immigrant from El Salvador, is both fascinating and thought provoking. I was particularly struck by the poem "Let Me Try Again." *Unaccompanied* was one of the first poetry books I read after joining Copper Canyon's board. This particular poem chronicles one of Javier's failed attempts to cross the US-Mexico border and paints a vivid picture of the situations he encountered. This poem gave me new insight and appreciation for the plight and determination of undocumented immigrants, and brought new meaning to the saying "If at first you don't succeed..."

RANDALL L. LANE, Board Member

On "Foreday in the Morning" by Jericho Brown

Jericho Brown's "Foreday in the Morning" stunned me the moment I read it, tears springing up like the morning glories referenced within. Jericho shines a light on the devastating consequences of neglecting acknowledgment and recognition. This poem is exquisite, heartbreaking and deeply powerful.

EMILY RAYMOND, Board Member

On "Bullet Points" by Jericho Brown

This powerful and evocative poem has haunted me ever since I first read it. The words, images, and fears that it conjures up have been, and are, the stuff of nightmares for many Black and Brown people in America, including me. The truth and tragic reality underlying Jericho's "Bullet Points" are frightening, uncomfortable, inescapable, and unforgettable. I consider it a meaningful must-read.

RANDALL L. LANE, Board Member

I found a copy of *Library of Small Catastrophes* in the Strand in 2019 and read it shortly before reading Eliot during a class on modernist poetry. This poem provided a road map for how I approach literature as a scholar, reader, and library worker, more aware of my fraught excitement about "our culture's haunted houses" and my reverence, or lack of it, for literary history.

REUBEN GELLEY NEWMAN, Intern

Self-Portrait of Librarian with T.S. Eliot's Papers

Alison C. Rollins
Library of Small Catastrophes (2019)

In the year 2020, T.S. Eliot's papers will be unsealed.
Let us go then, you and I. Let us take the dust in
our claws, lap the hundreds of letters spilling secrets
into the wasteland of our irreverent mouths.
Have we no couth? Have we not been trained
to know good things come to those who wait?
Each year we gather round the cave. We don our Sun-
day best, come to see what young muse has risen
from the dead. Tomorrow brings the past wrapped
in plastic eggs, the seal of history broken in present tense.
Storage units preserve our culture's haunted houses.
The canon is merely a ghost story. Write a poem *after* me
before I'm gone, and please do not include *rest in peace;*
only those who are forgotten go undisturbed, only things
kept in the dark know the true weight of light.

Recommended by **SHANGYANG FANG**, Poet

Romanticism (the Blue Keats)

Roger Reeves
King Me (2013)

I want a terrace of bamboo. A stuttering harp.
A garden fitted with a grotto and gimp hermit.
I want to lose my last name in the crickets
Coupling beneath my feet. I want the body's burden,
Four more angels to drag through the streets
Of a city that finds the monkey sacred, the fool careful,
The monk dumb. I want a painting of persimmons
And a persimmon. I want the violence of my love
To leave my sleep and my lover alone. I am dedicated
To the same baffled heart I have always carried.
The diamonds and mud of my mouth. The midsummer
Lurching toward the late-summer heat that will kill
The sage and tomato plants tanning on the veranda.
I want the water and the leg my uncle lost coming from the well.
If one body will hide another and call this hiding love,
I want to always torture myself with another's wet borders.
An ankle clicking against an ankle. The wrists fettered.
There was something I knew before this. Before my hands
Tore at the ropes, snapped cedar poles and ripped the silk
Of any tent I lay in. I want to know how the savage
Wind loves the house it destroys. I want to know before
I am both house and savage wind, before all of the tents
In the city become tattered rags snagged in the hair
Of our children and the redheaded trees. I am careful
To want nothing that I cannot lose and be sad in the losing.
A terrace made of rotting bamboo. A harp lost in its singing.
My last name and the tomatoes falling from the vine. Woman,
I want this plum heart. And the dying that makes us possible.

I love the second section of *Our Andromeda* for the playful way it engages with the conceit of parallel universes and multiple selves. It doesn't lose its eye for the poetic in the heady space of sci-fi, and, in "Visitor," that means we get to enter a familiar domestic scene and discover all its strangeness. I read this poem in one of my first workshops at George Mason, and Shaughnessy's speculative poems were an early lesson that poetry can be unstable, that we can be and not be ourselves in the same space.

TOBI KASSIM, Intern

Also recommended by **ELAINA ELLIS**, Editor

Visitor
Brenda Shaughnessy
Our Andromeda (2012)

I am dreaming of a house just like this one

but larger and opener to the trees, nighter

than day and higher than noon, and you,

visiting, knocking to get in, hoping for icy

milk or hot tea or whatever it is you like.

For each night is a long drink in a short glass.

A drink of blacksound water, such a rush

and fall of lonesome no form can contain it.

And if it isn't night yet, though I seem to

recall that it is, then it is not for everyone.

Did you receive my invitation? It is not

for everyone. Please come to my house

lit by leaf light. It's like a book with bright

pages filled with flocks and glens and groves

and overlooked by Pan, that seductive satyr

in whom the fish is also cooked. A book that

took too long to read but minutes to unread—

that is—to forget. Strange are the pages

thus. Nothing but the hope of company.

I made too much pie in expectation. I was

hoping to sit with you in a treehouse in a

nightgown in a real way. Did you receive

my invitation? Written in haste, before

leaf blinked out, before the idea fully formed.

An idea like a stormcloud that does not spill

or arrive but moves silently in a direction.

Like a dark book in a long life with a vague

hope in a wood house with an open door.

The *Selected Poems of Sándor Csoóri* is one of the earliest Copper Canyon books I have in my personal collection. I admire many poems in this book because Csoóri wrote poems to acknowledge the wisdom of rural life, and to defend that long-standing reality as it clashed with European modernism and the violence and silencing that came with it.

MAURICE MANNING, Poet

Green Twig in My Hand

Sándor Csoóri, translated from the Hungarian
by Len Roberts and Claudia Zimmerman
Selected Poems of Sándor Csoóri (1992)

Spring will turn frothy again
   like the mouth of the ever-singing bird,
and grass will grow around the mounds of earth,
      but you will not smile anymore
at anything that will be alive.

I will take a green twig to you, chicky catkin,
      beaming cowslips from beneath the mill-dam,
God's glance gleaming on them
      and the glance of the first bug crawling out into the world,
but you, drawing aside, just stare at the wall.

Who knows whether I will survive my incurable embarrassment,
   but I still want to remember even this last look in your eyes,
these eyes that burn black holes:
      sterile chalk-dust drifts into them
as though smashed Carthage's dust reached you only now.

I do not think death is more talented than me.
   I do not think death could take you away from me.
I can see myself in you as though I were sitting in a beautiful wound:
   green twig in my hand, and behind me, oh behind me,
vast spaces: all around me the otherworld darkening.

On "The Fountain" by Primus St. John

I bought St. John's 1999 book, *Communion,* in the used bookstore in the Raleigh-Durham International Airport many years ago. It sat on my shelf for a while before I read it, which I did while I was working on a series of essays on poetry and parenting. When I read the book, I was amazed at this important American voice that had been utterly unknown to me. From his landmark long poem "Dreamer"—perhaps the most significant poem about the trafficking of enslaved people since "Middle Passage"—to the unfinished poem that concludes the book, I heard someone who, in his nuanced approach to race, desire, and history, was way ahead of his time.

As I worked on an essay about these poems, I actually reached out to St. John, but the only way I could find to contact him was by mail. I found a likely address online and sent him a hard-copy letter. A few weeks later, there was an inimitable voice mail on my office phone—he signed off of the long message with his name, "Primus," and hung up, a move I think few could replicate convincingly. When I called back, he and I had a wonderful chat about his work, his life, and the poems. "The Fountain," from his first book, *Skins on the Earth* (1976), is one of my favorites of his—full of the pathos and philosophy that all of his work includes, but also full of a notable humor, which I love.

NATHANIEL PERRY, APR/Honickman First Book Prize winner

On *13th Balloon* by Mark Bibbins

When I first got to know Copper Canyon Press, in the early nineties, I would have been very surprised that a poem about the AIDS crisis, let alone one written by an openly gay poet, would be included in any of its books. Copper Canyon was decidedly heteronormative at that time—most presses were—but the AIDS crisis opened doors, for better or worse. The losses many of us experienced are near impossible to give voice to; the collective trauma we gay men lived through—the deaths of our brothers, our lovers, our friends, our family, our community—is real. Sometimes it takes decades to process it. Mark Bibbins's *13th Balloon* has the distance from that time to afford perspective that assuages a pain that never goes away.

IRA SILVERBERG, Board Member

✐ I remember excerpting *Soul Make a Path Through Shouting* as part of a condolences note to patrons of a museum I worked for—they had lost their only son to AIDS. They found the poem tender, thoughtful, and I know it made a difference for them. Poetry can allow us to note the difficult transitions in our lives, be they wonderful or terrible. This poem does that.

PATRICIA SPEARS JONES, Poet

Down from the Houses of Magic

Cyrus Cassells
Soul Make a Path Through Shouting (1994)

in Provincetown

I

Now the moon darns the moor with its fabric of minnows,
And the sea rushes with the ecstasy of ants.
Down from the houses of magic, a healing wind sweeps,
Down from the houses of magic.
On Gull Hill, in the flaming garden, God flings
A fistful of robin redbreasts—razzamatazz.
And the reed of the supple mind bends and shivers,
And the choirlike, match-stemmed, fiercely gallant flowers:
Johnny-jump-up, pert buttercup, anemone, peony, lupine,
The first lightning-white rose dying to open
Beneath the systole and diastole of starry night,
Iris, allium, the proffered chalices of tulips,
The colors of a fabulous dusk in Tunisia;
Coming soon, a pleasure of freesias, a pleasure.
Such tintinnabulation—listen:
All the prayer-wheels of April-into-May luster
Spinning God-drunk—till finally beside
The moon-daft willow, slack as a marionette,
The frenzy of scotch broom,
The fleet-souled orioles marshal, at wolf's hour,
Then sally in one brilliant will.

2

Abundance begins here—at the sea lip:
On the Cape I've come to God and Proteus, come to rest in wild places:
Whisker-still galaxies of marshlands,
Beaches where I pause and study

The Atlantic, teal and taciturn, the Atlantic, glittering and fluent,
As on blond days fishermen stagger
And bluefish wake to the breathless dream of land.

Having combed eerie dunes,
I have been on desolate moons, wind-worked to pure scrimshaw,
And found deer, cranberries, a plum dusk,
Pools of sweet water carved into sand.

The streets stink of fish, after the dark
Gimcrack shawls of squalls and rain.
I amble through rumors of shipwrecks, ghosts,
Sense the red broom-sweep of the beacon even in my sleep—

I have my tremendous window.
The moon-jacklit boat comes to it, shimmering,
And the bride-sweet cirrus cloud,
And sometimes the streak of a squirrel, like the deft, sudden
Stroke of the watercolorist, whose brush distills the bay.

And now, clear and fugitive, in jack-in-the-box brilliance,
The baby whale blooms:
Wild world, wild messenger—you are the moment's crown, sea-loved:
When providence brims to the outermost land,
No lack, no lack, but in my human mind—

3

Midsummer.
And after belligerent sun, twilight brings
A muezzin of sea-wind,
And the soul of the garden bows,
A praise in the earth:
Among Turk-cap lilies, suddenly,
In the willow's cool hair,
The breath of God—

Now I stand in the garden
Like a messenger proclaiming
I am Cyrus, and I am here,
Amid Lilliputian canon-flowers—
I surrender! I surrender!—
Under starry dippers pouring
Into a vast and holy dark—

4

One day on Gull Hill I wept and prayed:
Let this earth become a heaven—

Beyond the garden, the wall of clematis:
The world with its rills of blood,
The blue and virulent cell where a man was flayed
To make a flag of human skin—

Tonight the moon makes a silver threshing-floor of the sea.
Beside the moth-claimed path, the stone seraph decays,
The stiffened body of a finch—

The rose is no paraclete.
A keen star plummets into the heart's cup, the summer grasses.

And the blue earth resumes its measureless dialogue
Between catastrophe and plenty.

5

The dirty, nail-bitten hand
Of a Black Lear,
With the green and pink
Bracelets of a woman,
Inching its way
Through garbage:

Even in the garden on Gull Hill,
I see that hand:
All day rocking back and forth
Between Turk-cap lilies and the trash—
Till at last words spill out,
Ones I shrink from:

Are you hungry all the time?

Yes, all the time—

O grant us strength to fashion a table
Where each of us has a name—

6

From autumn to autumn, teach us
How to breathe, endure,
In the shadow of the sickening weapon;

Teach us how to blossom,
If the sky is acid,
The garden marred—

We move through the world with its drastic reds,
Its discord,
Seeking balm in all things:
Mother's milk, the dream of reunion—

Not enough to hate suffering,
Hate war,
But to jettison at last
All duality, division,
To discern
God-in-the-guise-of-the-stranger,
God-in-the-guise-of-this-flesh—

7

Then in my dream, like a hawk,
I circled the garden:
No, it was the Earth, the grand, lacerated Earth;
On its whorled surface,
All the ages of humankind.

And a voice sang:
Here are flowers of deep suffering,
Swaying in the heart of God—

8

Because
        Each of us must seek
A finer life, a finer death.

Because
        In the garden, beside clematis,
Jousting with slippery shadows
Of birth-and-death-and-birth-and-death,

Sometimes I come back to
The pitiless floor of Hiroshima,
Knowing in the terror and magnitude
Of true comprehension
I meant to die there—
Back to the fierce moment
After the *pika,* the flash,
When suddenly I reclaimed
A small, clear
Flicker of self—
My flesh gone,
But my soul still singing,
Adamant to live:

The history of survival is written under my lids.

9

And if the husk of the world is ripped away,

We will not have altered the consciousness of one leaf—

10

Let this earth become a heaven:
From the point of light within the mind of God,
The Earth hurling its roughhouse wills and lusters,
The Earth accruing poison—
Planet of joy, planet of crucifixion,
Piñata destined to be smashed—
Ashes, ashes,
All the mirrors of heaven blackening, imagine:
No lack, no lack, but in our human minds—

Let the clematis become a prayer
As clouds and canon-flowers ready
Sweet unguents of pollen and rain,
As God bellows, and a wild cavalry of wind sweeps
Down from the houses of magic
Down from the houses of magic
Down from the houses of magic

Why Copper Canyon?
So many translations
of Pablo Neruda !

1

2 Next 50 years
a poetry galaxy

My most worn CCP
book - Gregory Orr's
HOW BEAUTIFUL THE BELOVED

3

4

A line that sticks -
And is where space ends
Called death or infinity?

Review of my book -
not as important as
my gratitude to Sam Hamill

5

G
O
M
E

S
H
I
N
I
N
G

AMY
UYEMATSU

My first encounter with Copper Canyon was being gifted a copy of Ruth Stone's <u>In the Next Galaxy</u> from Borders bookstore which is now out of business! The cover's still life painting includes a <u>pear</u> which is an image that continues to echo in my mind's eye along with Stone's poems... ALISON C. ROLLINS

On "One of the Evenings" by James Richardson

"One of the Evenings" by James Richardson is pure mystery to me. I've tried to figure out why I return to it again and again. It's strange and familiar. It's quiet and it quickens along. It's sage and so specifically locked in the ordinary. It's just a feeling that "Yes. That's completely It."

HAILEY GAUNT, Intern

On "Sea Church" by Aimee Nezhukumatathil

Aimee Nezhukumatathil's "Sea Church" imbues me with delight and longing. The poem offers both childlike wonder and aching fragility. It is what I treasure most about poetry: an exquisite presentation of the tangible that contains layers of metaphor for emotion and experience.

JULIE CHRISTINE JOHNSON, Finance and Operations Manager

On "Reading Books" by Liu Tsung-yuan, translated from the Chinese by Red Pine

I read this poem during my summer internship at Copper Canyon and during a time I was reflecting on what poetry—both reading it and writing it—meant to me. More importantly, I was (re)considering why poetry mattered to my life, especially after a period of intense academic study during a series of global crises. Why does poetry matter? This poem re-aligned my whole way of thinking about reading literature, and especially poetry: "I yawn and stretch my limbs / I read out loud to my heart's content / I enjoy doing what suits me / not to please learned men."

I read poetry for many reasons—it opens my mind to new perspectives, it illuminates my spiritual self, it reinvigorates language, it changes the way a mind can think—but "Reading Books" reminds me that I read poetry first and foremost because it pleases me; poetry delights me. I can think of no better reason to keep it in my life.

KATE O'DONOGHUE, Intern

Fireworks in the sky and in the heart.

MICHAEL WIEGERS, Executive Editor

New Year's Eve

Xin Qiji, translated from the Chinese by Red Pine
Finding Them Gone: Visiting China's Poets of the Past (2016)

In the east wind last night a thousand trees burst forth
showered down
a rain of stars
jeweled horses and carriages and incense filled the road
the tremulous sound of a phoenix flute
the transforming glow of a jade vase
all night lanterns swayed
and she of the moth eyebrows and flower-decked hair
of laughter that beguiles and the subtlest of perfumes
whom I have searched for in crowds a hundred times
as I turned my head
she was there
where the lantern light was faint

The greatest poems may seem timeless, immortal, but they have this way of growing as we grow, dying as we die. This poem means far more to me now than it did when it first appeared a decade ago when Merwin was still alive.

TIMOTHY LIU, Poet

The Old Trees on the Hill

W.S. Merwin
The Shadow of Sirius (2008)

When you were living
and it was later than we knew
there was an old orchard
far up on the hill behind the house
dark apple trees wrapped in moss
standing deep in thorn bushes and wild grape
cobwebs breathing between the branches
memory lingering in silence
the spring earth fragrant with other seasons
crows conferred in those boughs and sailed on
chickadees talked of the place as their own
there were still kinglets and bluebirds
and the nuthatch following the folded bark
the churr of one wren a dark shooting star
with all that each of them knew then
but whoever had planted those trees
straightening now and again over the spade
to stand looking out across the curled
gleaming valley to the far gray ridges
one autumn after the leaves had fallen
while the morning frost still slept in the hollows
had been buried somewhere far from there
and those who had known him and his family
were completely forgotten you told me
and you said you had never been up there
though it was a place where you
loved to watch the daylight changing
and we looked up and watched the daylight there

Isatine Blues

Ed Pavlić
Paraph of Bone & Other Kinds of Blue (2001)

> *Why? It don't matter why.*
>
> Billie Holiday, "Deep Song"

Don't sing it
  to me. Or I'll stay under
    here motionless

& blue-gilled. I'll drift
  away from the shattered place
    of irruption.

Where the summer song
  crossed the winter street,
    the corner

where we met. & don't
  worry about me,
    I'll stick close

to pockets of air beneath
  the surface. Snatch shallow
    breaths of marrow

from bends in the death-blue
  shoulder blade of the ice patch.
    Go on & sing it,

just not to me. Last night,
  for a moment at rest
    on the keys,

I saw my finger tips melt
  chord prints into your frozen
    back. & Gershwin's

limo didn't come around
  to keep us honest. As you
    hummed changes

thru the tune the pockets
    of touch filled with water.
        & scarred

by warmth, they freeze again
    into glassy bullet wounds
        like transparent

Braille domes. My fingers
    slip off rounded keys;
        singularist,

I lose hold of you.
    & another song's gone
        off with the pale

frigoric voice, alight
    with the lilt of Southern
        flame.

Am I playing a player-
    piano? Behind the stool,
        a white veil wafts

as a bowl full of tangerine
    peels dries on a hissing radiator.
        Ancestress to burnt

lips on a scarlet trumpet,
    you turn body heat into liquid
        distance & back

to ice beneath my hands.
    Almost round, a charcoal sketch
        of a circle, we

dance underneath the ice,
    impaled by bolts of broken
        moonlight

we swayed in the tidal pull
    of silence. Sing to me now,
        rallentando down

to the sine qua non. Sing
    to me again & all last night
        & don't pause

at my fall away thru
  scented pillows & cloudless
    depths of the

sheets. Confess it
  this once, the uncanny
    chance.

The whetstone in your pocket
  & the unsheathed épée
    waved in your

voice. I stayed alert,
  but my whole body fell
    asleep. Round

about midnight & crescendo
  needles hold my limbs.
    Sing my forehead

back thru the eye
  of the needle or a
    millionth

of the mirror. Been under
  five minutes now, lungs ache
    & clutch, ears

drum a pressure rhythm
  to the echo-depth of time.
    If you're down,

stay down. & sing me back
  thru last night before I went
    touch-deaf

& ear-numb, before I melted
  at the edge of your lips
    & slipped beneath

the sand. & don't stop. Quiver-
  still, how the hands of a mesmerist
    work the future

out of fruit fallen from the Lychee
  tree. When you hum
    lightning

into Mera's "Higanbana,"
   a blue tree at the river bank burns
      orange, blown

in a red wind. Our storm tongues
   twist Madame Butterfly
      onto her mythic

back & summon a thunder-reaper
   with a Cutthroat on his
      shoulder. A mirror

image or a sure sign, a raven
   wears a ruby necklace,
      Amadina fasciata.

Splayed open down to our beating
   pit, two well ripened sinners
      washed up

onto broken glass & black coral
   of the soul's beach. I'm hanging
      on one muted line,

to touch the indigo heave
   of nightfall to the windward
      surf of cachexy.

If tone is homage to the pressure
   of secrets, sing to the numb
      spot, the nob

of bone growing behind my ear.
   Sing the warm spot that moves
      along my hip.

On "Ars Poetica" by Dana Levin

"Ars Poetica" from Dana Levin's *Wedding Day* became immensely important as I parented small kids and felt myself drifting from poetry, even as I had wholly new things to say in the landscape of motherhood. Levin's compact and vivid imagery, appalling and gorgeous, articulated exactly how it felt to need to write the poems that were not yet in the world. And maybe never would be.

REBECCA L. WEE, Poet

On "Memoir" by Dennis O'Driscoll

Reading the poem "Memoir," you can laugh and cry at the same time— at yourself and at the other in you— and when the poetry provokes not only psychological but also physical reactions, it cannot be forgotten.

LIDIJA DIMKOVSKA, Poet

On "Fragrance" by Ruth Stone

Ruth Stone's "Fragrance" seems alive, pulsating with the author's passion. These are not words on a page, but rather a palpable presence.

HEIDI J. SEWALL, Development Coordinator, Development Manager, and Development Administrator

On "Duplex: Cento" by Jericho Brown

I love the general badassery of this poem, the lack of apology. To be the other in someone's life, to have that other. The glory in the living of it.

RUTH GILA BERGER, Consortium Book Sales & Distribution Trade Sales Manager

This poem takes the hand, puts it on the heart, and, with a measure of melancholy, it gestures toward the affective dimension of human co-existence: neighborly friendship, mutual understandings, a recognition of decline that eschews humiliation out of empathy and kindness. These things don't have to be inscribed at all, or even spoken. But here they are, rendered in language—and, I suspect, done so almost as a meditation on language itself, on poetry. On a personal note, I do sentimentalize this poem's setting, the Northeast Kingdom—my beloved's from the area. What speaks to me above the strings of attachment is the remarkable poetic-attitudinal voice. That is what I seek out in art most of all: the artful yet sincere. Copper Canyon's made an entire catalogue out of it.

NICHOLAS SEOW, Intern

Marshall Washer

Hayden Carruth
Collected Shorter Poems, 1946–1991 (1992)

I

They are cowshit farmers, these New Englanders
who built our red barns so admired as emblems,
in photograph, in paint, of America's imagined
past (backward utopians that we've become).
But let me tell how it is inside those barns.
Warm. Even in dead of winter, even in the
dark night solid with thirty below, thanks
to huge bodies breathing heat and grain sacks
stuffed under doors and in broken windows, warm,
and heaped with reeking, steaming manure, running
with urine that reeks even more, the wooden channels
and flagged aisles saturated with a century's
excreta. In dim light, with scraper and shovel,
the manure is lifted into a barrow or a trolley
(suspended from a ceiling track), and moved
to the spreader—half a ton at a time. Grain
and hay are distributed in the mangers, bedding
of sawdust strewn on the floor. The young cattle
and horses, separately stabled, are tended. The cows
are milked; the milk is strained and poured
in the bulk tank; the machines and all utensils
are washed with disinfectant. This, which is called
the "evening chores," takes about three hours.
Next morning, do it again. Then after breakfast
hitch the manure spreader to the old Ferguson

and draw it to the meadows, where the manure
is kicked by mechanical beaters onto the snow.
When the snow becomes too deep for the tractor,
often about mid-January, then load the manure
on a horse-drawn sled and pitch it out by hand.
When the snow becomes too deep for the horses
make your dung heap behind the barn. Yes, a good
winter means no dung heap; but a bad one
may mean a heap as big as a house. And so,
so, night and morning and day, 365 days
a year until you are dead; this is part
of what you must do. Notice how many times
I have said "manure"? It is serious business.
It breaks the farmers' backs. It makes their land.
It is the link eternal, binding man and beast
and earth. Yet our farmers still sometimes say
of themselves, derogatively, that they are "cowshit
farmers."

2

        I see a man with a low-bent back
driving a tractor in stinging rain, or just as he
enters a doorway in his sheepskin and enormous
mittens, stomping snow from his boots, raising
his fogged glasses. I see a man in bib overalls
and rubber boots kneeling in cowshit to smear
ointment on a sore teat, a man with a hayfork,
a dungfork, an axe, a 20-pound maul
for driving posts, a canthook, a grease gun.
I see a man notching a cedar post
with a double-blade axe, rolling the post
under his foot in the grass: quick strokes and there
is a ringed groove one inch across, as clean
as if cut with the router blade down at the mill.
I see a man who drags a dead calf or watches
a barn roaring with fire and thirteen heifers
inside, I see his helpless eyes. He has stood
helpless often, of course: when his wife died
from congenital heart disease a few months before
open-heart surgery came to Vermont, when his sons
departed, caring little for the farm because
he had educated them—he who left school
in 1931 to work by his father's side
on an impoverished farm in an impoverished time.

I see a man who studied by lamplight, the journals
and bulletins, new methods, struggling to buy
equipment, forty years to make his farm
a good one; alone now, his farm the last
on Clay Hill, where I myself remember ten.
He says "I didn't mind it" for "I didn't notice it,"
"dreened" for "drained," "climb" (pronounced *climm*)
for "climbed," "stanchel" for "stanchion,"
and many other unfamiliar locutions; but I
have looked them up, they are in the dictionary,
standard speech of lost times. He is rooted
in history as in the land, the only man I know
who lives in the house where he was born. I see
a man alone walking his fields and woods,
knowing every useful thing about them, moving
in a texture of memory that sustains his lifetime
and his father's lifetime. I see a man
falling asleep at night with thoughts and dreams
I could not infer—and would not if I could—
in his chair in front of the television.

   3

                              I have written
of Marshall often, for his presence is in my poems
as in my life, so familiar that it is not named;
yet I have named him sometimes too, in writing
as in life, gratefully. We are friends. Our friendship
began when I came here years ago, seeking
what I had once known in southern New England,
now destroyed. I found it in Marshall, among others.
He is friend and neighbor both, an important
distinction. His farm is one-hundred-eighty acres
(plus a separate woodlot of forty more), and one
of the best-looking farms I know, sloping smooth
pastures, elm-shaded knolls, a brook, a pond,
his woods of spruce and pine, with maples and oaks
along the road—not a showplace, not by any means,
but a working farm with fences of old barbed wire;
no pickets, no post-and-rail. His cows are Jerseys.
My place, no farm at all, is a country laborer's
holding, fourteen acres "more or less" (as the deed
says), but we adjoin. We have no fence. Marshall's
cows graze in my pasture; I cut my fuel
in his woods. That's neighborliness. And when

I came here Marshall taught me . . . I don't know,
it seems like everything: how to run a barn,
make hay, build a wall, make maple syrup
without a trace of bitterness, a thousand things.
(Though I thought I wasn't ignorant when I came,
and I wasn't—just three-quarters informed.
You know how good a calf is, born three-legged.)
In fact half my life now, I mean literally half,
is spent in actions I could not perform without
his teaching. Yet it wasn't teaching; he *showed* me.
Which is what makes all the difference. In return
I gave a hand, helped in the fields, started
frozen engines, mended fence, searched for lost calves,
picked apples for the cider mill, and so on.
And Marshall, now alone, often shared my table.
This too is neighborliness.

4

As for friendship,
what can I say where words historically fail?
It is something else, something more difficult. Not
western affability, at any rate, that tells
in ten minutes the accommodation of its wife's—well,
you know. Yankees are independent, meaning
individual and strong-minded but also private;
in fact private first of all. Marshall and I
worked ten years together, and more than once
in hardship. I remember the late January
when his main gave out and we carried water,
hundreds and thousands of gallons, to the heifers
in the upper barn (the one that burned next summer),
then worked inside the well to clear the line
in temperatures that rose to ten below
at noonday. We knew such times. Yet never
did Marshall say the thought that was closest to him.
Privacy is what this is; not reticence, not
minding one's own business, but a positive sense
of the secret inner man, the sacred identity.
A man is his totem, the animal of his mind.
Yet I was angered sometimes. How could friendship
share a base so small of mutual substance?
Unconsciously I had taken friendship's measure
from artists elsewhere who had been close to me,
people living for the minutest public dissection

of emotion and belief. But more warmth was,
and is, in Marshall's quiet "hello" than in all
those others and their wordiest protestations,
more warmth and far less vanity.

5

                              He sows
his millet broadcast, swinging left to right,
a half-acre for the cows' "fall tonic" before
they go in the barn for good; an easy motion,
slow swinging, a slow dance in the field, and just
the opposite, right to left, for the scythe
or the brush-hook. Yes, I have seen such dancing
by a man alone in the slant of the afternoon.
At his anvil with his big smith's hammer
he can pound shape back in a wagon iron, or tap
a butternut so it just lies open. When he skids
a pine log out of the woods he stands in front
of his horse and hollers, "Gee-up, goddamn it,"
"Back, you ornery son-of-a-bitch," and then
when the chain rattles loose and the log settles
on the stage, he slicks down the horse's sweaty
neck and pulls his ears. In October he eases
the potatoes out of the ground in their rows,
gentle with the potato-hook, then leans and takes
a big one in his hand, and rubs it clean
with his thumbs, and smells it, and looks
along the new-turned frosty earth to fields,
to hills, to the mountain, forests in their color
each fall no less awesome. And when in June
the mowing time comes around and he fits the wicked
cutter-bar to the Ferguson, he shuts the cats
indoors, the dogs in the barn, and warns
the neighbors too, because once years ago,
many years, he cut off a cat's legs in the tall
timothy. To this day you can see him
squirm inside when he tells it, as he must tell it,
obsessively, June after June. He is tall,
a little gray, a little stooped, his eyes
crinkled with smile-lines, both dog-teeth gone.
He has worn his gold-rimmed spectacles so long
he looks disfigured when they're broken.

6

No doubt
Marshall's sorrow is the same as human
sorrow generally, but there is this
difference. To live in a doomed city, a doomed
nation, a doomed world is desolating, and we all,
all are desolated. But to live on a doomed farm
is worse. It must be worse. There the exact
point of connection, gate of conversion, is—
mind and life. The hilltop farms are going.
Bottomland farms, mechanized, are all that survive.
As more and more developers take over
northern Vermont, values of land increase,
taxes increase, farming is an obsolete vocation—
while half the world goes hungry. Marshall walks
his fields and woods, knowing every useful thing
about them, and knowing his knowledge useless.
Bulldozers, at least of the imagination,
are poised to level every knoll, to strip bare
every pasture. Or maybe a rich man will buy it
for a summer place. Either way the link
of the manure, that had seemed eternal, is broken.
Marshall is not young now. And though I am only
six or seven years his junior, I wish somehow
I could buy the place, merely to assure him
that for these few added years it might continue—
drought, flood, or depression. But I am too
ignorant, in spite of his teaching. This is more
than a technocratic question. I cannot smile
his quick sly Yankee smile in sorrow,
nor harden my eyes with the true granitic resistance
that shaped this land. How can I learn the things
that are not transmissible? Marshall knows them.
He possesses them, the remnant of human worth
to admire in this world, and I think to envy.

Recommended by **KRIS BECKER**,
Development Manager and Office
Manager

Lilac Time

Hayden Carruth
Scrambled Eggs & Whiskey: Poems 1991–1995 (1996)

The winter was fierce, my dear,
    Snowy and blowy and cold,
A heart-breaker and record-breaker,
    And I am feeble and old.

But now it is lilac time.
    Come out in the sweet warm air,
Come and I'll gather flowers
    To put in your beautiful hair.

Let's make a bouquet of lilac
    For our old bedside table.
Then the fragrance in the night
    Will make me form-i-dable.

On "For Jan, with Love" by David Lee

Sometimes we die in the middle of delivering our genetic message. Sometimes people will bet on whether or not you survive. All these years later, I still love the figure of Jan from David Lee's "For Jan, with Love," but now even more so. With her small hands she tries to make a difference where no difference can be made. I think she tries harder than the rest and that's why it's her poem.

JOSH BELL, Poet

On "Words, of course, but" by Gregory Orr

I love the simplicity and plain speech Orr uses, and in "Words, of course, but," he reminds us of our need for silence and the unspoken—including the silence that inhabits our poems.

AMY UYEMATSU, Poet

On "Mother" by Ted Kooser

Every poem in *Delights & Shadows* is exceptionally splendid. "Mother" is a poem I have memorized because of the subtle way it moves from image to image, with liquidity and lyricism, and because of the way it builds to an ending that strikes me profoundly. There's a sobriety in the great honor of this work, the quiet love. As well, it gives me the overwhelming sensation that many have tried to describe— but, really, it's not at all like the top of my head was taken off. It's more like I've seen someone befriend a wolf. How is it possible for a human to get that close to something so wild?

CONNIE WANEK, Poet

Kooser can find a metaphor for almost anything. This poem is a classic
example of that.

JIM HEYNEN, Poet

Memory

Ted Kooser
Delights & Shadows (2004)

Spinning up dust and cornshucks
as it crossed the chalky, exhausted fields,
it sucked up into its heart
hot work, cold work, lunch buckets,
good horses, bad horses, their names
and the names of mules that were
better or worse than the horses,
then rattled the dented tin sides
of the threshing machine, shook
the manure spreader, cranked
the tractor's crank that broke
the uncle's arm, then swept on
through the windbreak, taking
the treehouse and dirty magazines,
turning its fury on the barn
where cows kicked over buckets
and the gray cat sat for a squirt
of thick milk in its whiskers, crossed
the chicken pen, undid the hook,
plucked a warm brown egg
from the meanest hen, then turned
toward the house, where threshers
were having dinner, peeled back
the roof and the kitchen ceiling,
reached down and snatched up
uncles and cousins, grandma, grandpa,
parents and children one by one,
held them like dolls, looked
long and longingly into their faces,
then set them back in their chairs
with blue and white platters of chicken
and ham and mashed potatoes
still steaming before them, with
boats of gravy and bowls of peas
and three kinds of pie, and suddenly,

⌐ I love that Copper Canyon Press's reach is worldwide. This poem was
written by a Vietnamese poet two hundred years ago, and her work is very
much alive in English because the Press's founders recognized the essential
work of translation—a value we strive to continue to recognize today.

JOHN BALABAN, Poet and Translator

Spring-Watching Pavilion

Hồ Xuân Hương, translated from the Nôm by John Balaban
Spring Essence: The Poetry of Hồ Xuân Hương (2000)

A gentle spring evening arrives
airily, unclouded by worldly dust.

Three times the bell tolls echoes like a wave.
We see heaven upside down in sad puddles.

Love's vast sea cannot be emptied.
And springs of grace flow easily everywhere.

Where is nirvana?
Nirvana is here, nine times out of ten.

The City of the Olesha Fruit

Norman Dubie
The Mercy Seat: Collected & New Poems 1967–2001 (2001)

for Barry Goldensohn

The spider vanished at the boy's mere
Desire to touch it with his hand.

Yuri Olesha

Outside the window past the two hills there is the city
Where the color-blind are waking to blue pears;
Also, there are the blue treetops waving
To the schoolgirls who step harshly along
In winter dresses: out of the mouths of these girls
Come the cones, their breath,
A mist like the silver ear trumpets
Of deaf children tipped toward whatever it is
They are almost hearing.

An old man without legs, not yet in a chair, has
Invented the city outside the window.
And everywhere now it is morning! He hears

His wife climbing the stairs.
What, he thinks . . . what to do?
The strong line of her back
Is like a spoon.
He says, "Good morning and how are you?"
She says, "Rumen,
I told you the hen should have been put
Up with straw in the attic. Last night the fox
Ate all of her but the dark spurs under the chin
And a few feathers."

His wife gathers him up in her arms, walks to the far
Corner of the room, and lowers him into a straight chair
Beside a table. Only last year he would sit
And stare at the shoes he could wear, without socks

And with the laces loose.
A tub is filling in another room.

He thinks, "Poor Widow is inside the stomach
Of a fox. My wife's idea was not a good one:
Where would Widow have found the scratch
And gravel for her shells while up in the attic?
And what about
The rooster! What about the poor rooster
On his railing by the barn; inconsolable, crowing?"
Rumen remembers a Russian story about a copper rooster
With a green fern for a tail.
Rumen's favorite writer is the great Russian
Yuri Olesha. Rumen thinks, "Yes, Yuri, my companion,
There is cruelty in the format of a kiss!
And the blue skins of pears
In a heap on a dish leave a memory

Of myself as a boy running along the flume water
Down past the village ditch.
But, Yuri, in my city all the streets are,
Just this moment, being swept: old women
In jade dresses sweeping, sweeping.
And soon it will rain for them and then
I'll return their sun, a noon sun
To take away the wet before the children
Rush out under the bells for an hour's recess.

Oh, Yuri, just beyond the grin of a smelly
Old fox, that's where Widow is, our best hen!
Yuri, my legs, I think, are buried in the orchard
Beside the stable where the hospital horses
Of my city wait, poised for an emergency.
These horses are constant; how they race
Down the cobbled streets for me. They've never
Trampled the children!"

"Rumen," his wife called, "do you want a haircut
This morning?" She steps into the room.

He smiles at her. She is buttoning her blouse.
And she smiles back to him. Rumen would say

To Yuri that sometimes her yellow hair
Got into the corners of his mouth.

"And, Yuri, that was when I most missed my youth."
Then Rumen would again fall silent.
He was off opening a raincloud over his city.
It was winter when he woke, but now I'm sure it's
Not. There are a few dark flowers?
Rumen feels that it is best for the children
If they walk to school in the clear winter air, but
Once he gets around to raining on his trees,
Streets, and houses, well, then he changes everything
To late July or August.
But the evenings in his city are always
Placed in autumn: there is the smell
Of woodsmoke, so pleasant,
And leaves burning. Flocks of bluebirds would be
Flying south.

And so there is the obscurity of many lives,
Not yours, Olesha, but mine and my wife's,
Two characters
Who are, perhaps, in a shade
Just now sipping an iced summer tea
With its twigs and leaves floating around inside:

We are giggling, I think, about how shy
We were as lovers that first winter night
When I kissed her in the dark barn
Right in her open eye. I tried again
And missed again. To accidentally kiss a young girl

In her open eye is, I think,
The beginning of experience. *Yuri,*
I did find her mouth that night!

But then the following winter, a week before
Our wedding, I missed again, this time
I kissed a small bare breast.
That wasn't an accident—

She reached out to touch my hand
And found my thigh!
The shyness of lovers, as softly, at night,
They miss and miss while following an old map, yes,
The format of a kiss.
In the city of the Olesha fruit

A citizen never dies, he just wakes
One morning without his legs, and then he is given
A city of his very own making:

In this way his existence narrows
While expanding like a diary, or
Like this landscape with two hills
Seen through my window early
Each and every winter morning! But, Yuri,
Outside this window—yes, I know,

What's there is there, and all of it
Indelible as our memory of blue pears, washed
And being eaten in the sunlight of a city
That is being constructed all of the time,
Its new gold domes and towers,
Just beyond two hills in the winter air, and
Somewhere inside the mind.

Bob Hicok is one of the greats. Thank you for continuing the essential work of publishing him.

MATTHEW ZAPRUDER, Poet

Don't say a word

Bob Hicok
Sex & Love & (2016)

Strange to be alive. I say that
in the conviction I was once a rock.
Living in the mountains
is coming home. Maybe, but the maple
is shaking no. I like the narcissism
of wind better than my own. Do trees dream

of walking away? I'd love to stand
in one place and give oxygen to the sky
to give life to you. If I die today,
this is my last poem. What have I done—
overused *love*. I won't recognize silence,
even when silence is all I've become.

On "[The ship] is slowly giving up her sentient life. I cannot write about it" by Jean Valentine

Jean Valentine's poems wash shame from the body. I imagine this one like the big, heavy sponge the birds lift in the cartoon *Cinderella*.

CHESSY NORMILE, APR/Honickman First Book Prize winner

The beauty and wonder of Jean Valentine's poetry, for me, has to do with the way her images always contain a kernel of familiarity no matter how deeply they live in her dreams. This poem touches so many corners of feeling—the impending loss of a loved one, the sadness and aliveness of love ("My scalp is alive / love touched it"), and the beauty of being briefly able to live beyond the self.

TOBI KASSIM, Intern

On "In the Mansion of Happiness" by C.D. Wright

Everyone who's changed their home knows the inner, unspoken, silent scream of the human self: I want to go home. The crucial statement in this poem is "Don't ask," and C.D. Wright doesn't ask because she feels, sees, knows, and writes.

LIDIJA DIMKOVSKA, Poet

On "Yes, Think" by Ruth Stone

This poem is all of life in thirteen sweet lines. It's among my go-to poems whenever I'm lucky enough to share poems with an uninitiated. May it live on forever.

JOSH HAMILTON, Intern

On "Green" by Laura Kasischke

I love that this poem honors minor tragedies, that it takes as a given that life is worthwhile in spite of its barrage of tragedies.

ELIZABETH O'BRIEN, Consortium Book Sales & Distribution
Inside Sales Representative

On "Little Voice" by Matthew Zapruder

I can't read "Little Voice" without remembering Matthew reading it or remembering a film of Matthew reading it. The memory may or may not be what happened, but in this film he's wearing a bruised tan jacket and a black stocking cap, blown-out jeans, and we're either in the red stones of James Turrell's Roden Crater or behind some civic auditorium in Santa Cruz or in a parking lot in Providence, but Matthew is standing in the center of the frame, reading these words very carefully, enunciating each syllable precisely to bring the viewers, the readers, and listeners into the eviscerated zone of poetry, where his voice becomes the silent voice that reads along in our heads when we're really finally reading a poem, falling off the end of the line only to rise back up just so, the mind the white paper and the black lines perfectly forming a thought you didn't know you had before. The poem ends. The filmmaker retreats on his skateboard, a tunneling glide with Matthew still at the center, looking at the poem, deeply puzzled by what's just happened there, brought on by the little voice made manifest and gone again.

TRAVIS NICHOLS, Poet

⌐ The best poems transform the ordinary into something extraordinary,
something memorable, indelible.

TIMOTHY LIU, Poet

The Cabbage

Ruth Stone
In the Next Galaxy (2002)

You have rented an apartment.
You come to this enclosure with physical relief,
your heavy body climbing the stairs in the dark,
the hall bulb burned out, the landlord
of Greek extraction and possibly a fatalist.
In the apartment leaning against one wall,
your daughter's painting of a large frilled cabbage
against a dark sky with pinpoints of stars.
The eager vegetable, opening itself
as if to eat the air, or speak in cabbage
language of the meanings within meanings;
while the points of stars hide their massive
violence in the dark upper half of the painting.
You can live with this.

I've loved this poem ever since I read it as a production intern at Copper Canyon. I'd ended a relationship just a few months before my internship started, and another one ended about eight months afterward. In both relationships, we'd fallen hard and fast for each other. Death and violence felt like a constant threat, which might be an experience shared by queer couples. These relationships felt deeper, more frightening, more terrible than I could have ever imagined.

Rekdal's poem captures all of these feelings and contrasts them with the stories we've told ourselves of the Greek gods: their jealousy, their lust, their fickle desires, their craving for power and dominance above all else. This poem captures exactly what makes our mortal, human love so precious: we love deeply, we love swiftly, we cherish and cling to these fragile, beautiful, terrifying connections, because we know in our hearts that our time on this earth is limited. We are not gods. We cannot live forever. So we live as best we can, we love as best we can, for as long as we can in this lifetime.

RON MARTIN-DENT, Intern

Mortal Love
Paisley Rekdal
Imaginary Vessels (2016)

If we were immortal, the poet said, like
the Greek gods, love
would not be needed because time
ceases to matter: love
needs urgency to be felt at all,

at which point I left the hall, hurrying
home to cook us dinner and change the sheets,
to sit a moment and rest
before you came back home to me, thinking

all the time of the gods in our stories who, even
with eternity to spare, loved,

which brought them into the human
realms of war and murder, the chaining
of lesser beings in pits of flame, the skinning
of rivals, and the creation of children

sometimes beautiful, sometimes monstrous:
the need for the shapes and skins of animals
to disguise their desires, meaning

the gods knew guilt too, and shame,
and jealousy; they knew, as we tell ourselves, about all
the human emotions in which love

is rooted: self-love and love
for spouses, daughters, sons, other
people's wives; the love for ex-
lovers too, those secret

old needs flamed out but the ashes nursed
out of respect for the failure. The gods loved

because we wanted them to be like us: no,
it is not an excess of time
that would keep them from feeling it: love
embroiders time—moving in and out of what
we imagine of it or what, if we were gods,
we could finally know.

For them, death is the thing
that is expendable; eternity means only
that suffering can be withstood
because it may be forgotten, because we are the ones
who must exist in the quick

sharpening and dulling of whatever wounds
assert us as human.

                      If we are different from the gods,
it is because we are more afraid, our sweet,
dim ordinary pleasures necessary
to assuage what can't be forgotten, an instinct
where theirs is an indulgence, and so our love

is deeper, more frightening, more terrible
than theirs. The gods loved, but they loved only

as *like us* as they could. They could never match it,
they would never match it, and it is because

of all the things they loved,
eternity would teach them to covet most
their power and their will.

We have these things too, in abundance.
But not time. For love
needs no time at all.

I THANK THE LATE JIM HARRISON
FOR INTRODUCING MY POEMS TO
COPPER CANYON BY TAKING OUR
COLLABORATION, BRAIDED CREEK
TO THE PRESS. JIM WAS A GENEROUS
AND SOMETIMES FORCEFUL ADVOCATE
AND I FOLLOWED HIS LEAD BY FORWARD-
ING MANUSCRIPTS BY CONNIE WANEK
AND NATALIE DIAZ. IT'S BEEN AN HONOR
TO BE PART OF THIS GREAT COMMUNION
OF POETS. —— TED KOOSER

In a gloomy city far from home, I read
"Memory" aloud to my sister and mother
as the answer to the question "Why
poetry." Afterwards for long minutes
we sat in silence. My mother sighed.
Then rain began to empty the sky,
and the whirlwind moved on.
Delights and Shadows by Ted Kooser.
     (offered by Connie Wanek)
                                    11/7/22

Index of Poets and Translators

Index of Poem Titles

Contributors

We are grateful to the Copper Canyon community members who contributed their favorite poems, personal stories, handwritten notes, and photographs to the making of this book.

Kelli Russell Agodon
Poet since 2021

Jay Aja
Intern, winter/spring 2023

Zuhra Amini
Intern, fall 2020

Janeen Armstrong
Intern Program Manager since 2017
Reader Services Manager since 2015

James Arthur
Poet since 2012

Jenny Rae Bailey
Intern, winter 2011

Jay Baker
Intern, fall 2022

John Balaban
Poet and Translator since 1991

Willis Barnstone
Poet since 2003

Ellen Bass
Poet since 2007

Kris Becker
Development Manager, 2004–2008
Office Manager and Development
Assistant, 2001–2004

Joseph Bednarik
Copublisher since 2016
Marketing Director, 1998–2016

Erin Belieu
Poet since 1995

Josh Bell
Poet since 2016

Donna Bellew
Board Member since 2015

Ruth Gila Berger
Consortium Book Sales &
Distribution Trade Sales Manager

Linda Bierds
Poet since 2019

Jeffrey Bishop
Board Member since 2016

Ellie Black
Intern, spring 2019

Jacob Boles
Intern, winter/spring 2017

Jaswinder Bolina
Poet since 2023

Marianne Boruch
Poet since 2011

David Bottoms
Poet since 1995

Geoff Bouvier
Poet since 2005

Heather Brennan
Intern, summer 2018

Valerie Brewster Caldwell
Book and Collateral Designer,
1995–2018

Nellie Bridge
Letterpress Printer, 1998–2002
Intern, winter/spring 1999

Traci Brimhall
Poet since 2017

Joan M. Broughton
Former Financial Consultant

Olga Broumas
Poet and Translator since 1989

Jeffrey Brown
Poet since 2015

Josh Brown
Consortium Book Sales &
Distribution Operations and
Metadata Supervisor

Elizabeth Brueggemann
Intern, winter/spring 2023

Laura Buccieri
Director of Publicity, 2017–2021

Vincent Buck
Board Member since 2014

David Caligiuri
Copyeditor and Proofreader since
1996

Kayleb Rae Candrilli
Poet since 2021

Cyrus Cassells
Poet since 1994

Sarah Cavanaugh
Board Member, 2005–2009

Thomas Centolella
Poet since 1990

Elizabeth J. Coleman
Editor of *Here: Poems for the Planet*
(2019)

Christie Collins
Editorial Assistant, 2013–2016
Intern, summer 2011

Alfred Corn
Poet since 2008

Tyree Daye
Poet since 2017
2017 APR/Honickman First Book
Prize winner

Jackie Delaney
Intern, summer 2017

Alex Dimitrov
Poet since 2017

Lidija Dimkovska
Poet since 2012

Tishani Doshi
Poet since 2012

Catherine Edwards
Board Member, 2003–2006

Elaina Ellis
Editor, 2012–2022

Laurie Eustis
Board Member, 2017–2020

Kerry James Evans
Poet since 2013

Shangyang Fang
Poet since 2021

Sascha Feinstein
Poet since 2000

Roz Anderson Flood
Board Member since 2020

Bob Francis
Volunteer, 2006–2020

Angela Garbes
Publicist, 2005–2007
Intern, summer 1999

Hailey Gaunt
Intern, fall 2019

Dan Gerber
Poet since 2007

Sierra Golden
Intern, fall 2012–winter 2013

Roger Greenwald
Translator since 2001

James Gregorski
Intern, fall 2009–winter 2010

Josh Hamilton
Intern, winter/spring 2018

Art Hanlon
Associate Editor of *The Complete Poems of Kenneth Rexroth* (2006)
Volunteer, 2001–2006
Intern, fall 1998–summer 2001

Clayton Haselwood
Intern, fall 2012

Lilah Hegnauer
Poet since 2005

Jim Heynen
Poet since 1981

Scott Hightower
Poet since 2005

Claretta Holsey
Production Editor since 2021
Intern, spring 2021

David Huerta
Poet since 2009

Maria Hummel
2013 APR/Honickman First Book Prize winner

Mark Irwin
Reader and Educator

Julie Christine Johnson
Finance and Operations Manager since 2021

Patricia Spears Jones
Poet since 2023

Richard Jones
Poet since 1991

Tobi Kassim
Intern, fall 2022

Asela Lee Kemper
Intern, fall 2021

Richard Kenney
Board Member, 1996–1999

Mary Jane Knecht
Development Director, 2001–2004
Managing Editor, 1984–1993

George Knotek
Copublisher since 2016
Development Director, 2008–2016

Jennifer L. Knox
Poet since 2020

Ted Kooser
Poet since 2004

Phil Kovacevich
Pressmark Designer, 2023
Book Designer since 2000

Randall L. Lane
Board Member since 2017

Laurel Larson-Harsch
Intern, fall 2019

David Lee
Poet since 1978

Dana Levin
Poet since 1999
1999 APR/Honickman First Book
Prize winner

Peter Lewis
Acting Publisher, 2002–2003
Board Member, 1996–2003

Gary Copeland Lilley
Poet since 2008

Timothy Liu
Poet since 1995

Noah Lloyd
Intern, winter/spring 2012

Alison Lockhart
Copyeditor and Proofreader since
2011
Editorial Assistant, 2008–2011
Intern, spring 2007

Maurice Manning
Poet since 2017

Ivy Marie
Intern, winter/spring 2023

Ron Martin-Dent
Intern, winter/spring 2016

Ellie Mathews
The North Press Letterpress Printer

Heather McHugh
Poet since 2009

Kelly McLennon
Intern, fall 2019

Hannah Messinger
Intern, fall 2018

Philip Metres
Poet since 2020

Jane Miller
Poet since 1993

Tyler Mills
Reader and Educator

Roger Mitchell
Poet since 2008

Tomás Q. Morín
Poet and Translator since 2012

Kate Morley
Intern, fall 2011

Valzhyna Mort
Poet since 2008

Justin Nash
Intern, summer 2019

Emmy Newman
Intern, winter/spring 2018

Reuben Gelley Newman
Intern, fall 2020

Aimee Nezhukumatathil
Poet since 2018

Travis Nichols
Poet since 2010

Chessy Normile
2020 APR/Honickman First Book
Prize winner

Elizabeth O'Brien
Consortium Book Sales &
Distribution Inside Sales
Representative

William O'Daly
Poet and Translator since 1979
Press Cofounder

Kate O'Donoghue
Intern, summer 2021

Lisa Olstein
Poet since 2006

David Orr
Poet since 2018

Eric Pankey
Poet since 2003

Walter Parsons
Board Member, 2002–2011

Ed Pavlić
Poet since 2001

Peter Pereira
Poet since 2003

Nathaniel Perry
2011 APR/Honickman First Book
Prize winner

John Pierce
Managing Editor, 2017–2022
Copyeditor and Proofreader, 2009–
2017

Red Pine
Translator since 1983

Kevin Prufer
Poet since 2023

Alicia Jo Rabins
Poet since 2015

Janna Rademacher
Consortium Book Sales &
Distribution Client Relations
Manager

Dean Rader
Poet since 2017

Natasha Rao
2021 APR/Honickman First Book
Prize winner

Emily Raymond
Board Member since 2017

James Richardson
Poet since 2001

Joseph C. Roberts
Board Member since 2007

Sam Robison
Intern, fall 2018

Alison C. Rollins
Poet since 2019

David Romtvedt
Poet since 1992

Tonaya Rosenberg
Managing Editor, 2011–2017

Wesley Rothman
Intern, summer 2011

Larry Rouch
Board Member, 2001–2005 and
2011–2016

Elizabeth Rush
Intern, summer 2006

Lily Sadighmehr
Intern, winter/spring 2020

Jacob Saenz
2018 APR/Honickman First Book
Prize winner

Tina Schumann
Grant Writer, 2007–2008
Intern, summer 2007

Kim Brown Seely
Board Member since 2014

Nicholas Seow
Intern, winter/spring 2014

Heidi J. Sewall
Development Coordinator since 2023
Development Manager, 2021–2023
Development Administrator, 2018–
2021

Natalie Shapero
Poet since 2017

Ira Silverberg
Board Member since 2019

Maurya Simon
Poet since 1986

Ed Skoog
Poet since 2009

Monica Sok
Poet since 2020

Christopher Soto
Poet since 2022

Arendt Speser
Editorial Assistant, 2002–2003

Melissa Stein
Poet since 2010
2010 APR/Honickman First Book
Prize winner

Tree Swenson
Press Cofounder

Arthur Sze
Poet and Translator since 1995

Peter Szilagyi
Intern, summer 2020

Kaci X. Tavares
Development Manager since 2023
Publishing Fellow, 2022–2023
Intern, winter/spring 2022

Elaine Terranova
Poet since 1995

Chase Twichell
Poet and Translator since 2003

Azura Tyabji
Intern, fall 2022

Amy Uyematsu
Poet since 2005

Jeremy Voigt
Website Proofreader, fall 2000
Intern, summer 2000

Corey Van Landingham
Reader and Book Reviewer

Dan Waggoner
Board Member since 2009

Connie Wanek
Poet since 2010

Sanna Wani
Intern, fall 2021

Emily Warn
Poet since 1982
Acting Publisher, 2002–2003
Board Member, 1998–2002

Noah Warren
Poet since 2021

Michael Wasson
Poet since 2022

Rebecca L. Wee
Poet since 2001

Eliot Weinberger
Translator since 1992

Michael White
Poet since 1992

Michael Wiegers
Executive Editor since 2002
Managing Editor, 1993–2002

Cole W. Williams
Intern, fall 2021

Gail Wronsky
Poet since 2000

Ashley E. Wynter
Editor since 2022

Ryo Yamaguchi
Publicist since 2021

Matthew Zapruder
Poet since 2006

About the Editors

Michael Wiegers is the Executive Editor of Copper Canyon Press, where, over the past three decades, he has edited and published more than five hundred titles. He additionally serves as Poetry Editor for *Narrative* magazine. Wiegers edited *A House Called Tomorrow: Fifty Years of Poetry from Copper Canyon Press* and two retrospective volumes of the poetry of Frank Stanford, *What About This* (a finalist for the 2015 National Book Critics Circle Award) and *Hidden Water* (with Chet Weise). He is also the editor of *Reversible Monuments: Contemporary Mexican Poetry* (with Mónica de la Torre), *The Poet's Child,* and *This Art: Poems about Poetry.* He lives in Port Townsend, Washington, and is writing a book about W.S. Merwin.

Kaci X. Tavares is a bilingual poet and editor from Honolulu, Hawaiʻi. She is currently Copper Canyon Press's Development Manager and was recently a writing mentor with the New York–based nonprofit Girls Write Now. With the University of East Anglia Publishing Project, she coedited the *UEA MA Poetry Anthology 2020* (Egg Box Publishing) and has edited feature-length and cultural short film scripts. She holds degrees in English and English education from Boston University and an MA in creative writing from the University of East Anglia. She lives in Washington state with her family.

Poetry is vital to language and living. Since 1972, Copper Canyon Press has published extraordinary poetry from around the world to engage the imaginations and intellects of readers, writers, booksellers, librarians, teachers, students, and donors.

WE ARE GRATEFUL FOR THE MAJOR SUPPORT PROVIDED BY:

academy of american poets

THE PAUL G. ALLEN FAMILY FOUNDATION

 amazon literary partnership

 POETRY FOUNDATION

4 CULTURE

Lannan

 the point envision·enact·evolve

  National Endowment for the Arts arts.gov
ART WORKS.

 WASHINGTON STATE ARTS COMMISSION

 A& OFFICE OF ARTS & CULTURE SEATTLE

 The Witter Bynner Foundation for Poetry

TO LEARN MORE ABOUT UNDERWRITING
COPPER CANYON PRESS TITLES,
PLEASE CALL 360-385-4925 EXT. 103

WE ARE GRATEFUL FOR THE MAJOR SUPPORT PROVIDED BY:

Richard Andrews and
   Colleen Chartier
Anonymous
Jill Baker and Jeffrey Bishop
Anne and Geoffrey Barker
Donna Bellew
Will Blythe
John Branch
Diana Broze
John R. Cahill
Sarah Cavanaugh
Keith Cowan and Linda Walsh
Stephanie Ellis-Smith and
   Douglas Smith
Mimi Gardner Gates
Gull Industries Inc.
   on behalf of William True
William R. Hearst III
Carolyn and Robert Hedin
David and Jane Hibbard
Bruce S. Kahn
Phil Kovacevich and Eric Wechsler

Lakeside Industries Inc.
   on behalf of Jeanne Marie Lee
Maureen Lee and Mark Busto
Ellie Mathews and Carl Youngmann
   as The North Press
Larry Mawby and Lois Bahle
Hank and Liesel Meijer
Petunia Charitable Fund and
   adviser Elizabeth Hebert
Madelyn S. Pitts
Suzanne Rapp and Mark Hamilton
Adam and Lynn Rauch
Emily and Dan Raymond
Joseph C. Roberts
Cynthia Sears
Kim and Jeff Seely
D.D. Wigley
Barbara and Charles Wright
In honor of C.D. Wright,
   from Forrest Gander
Caleb Young as C. Young Creative
The dedicated interns and faithful
   volunteers of Copper Canyon Press

The pressmark for Copper Canyon Press suggests
entrance, connection, and interaction
while holding at its center
an attentive, dynamic space for poetry.

This book is set in Apolline Std.
Cover design by Phil Kovacevich.
Book design and composition by Claretta Holsey.
Printed on archival-quality paper.